Brooke Foss Westcott

The Gospel of Life

Thoughts introductory to the study of Christian doctrine. Second Edition

Brooke Foss Westcott

The Gospel of Life
Thoughts introductory to the study of Christian doctrine. Second Edition

ISBN/EAN: 9783337095413

Printed in Europe, USA, Canada, Australia, Japan

Cover: Foto ©Lupo / pixelio.de

More available books at **www.hansebooks.com**

THE GOSPEL OF LIFE:

THOUGHTS INTRODUCTORY TO THE STUDY OF CHRISTIAN DOCTRINE.

BY

BROOKE FOSS WESTCOTT, D.D., D.C.L.,

BISHOP OF DURHAM ;
FORMERLY REGIUS PROFESSOR OF DIVINITY, CAMBRIDGE.

SECOND EDITION.

London :

MACMILLAN AND CO.

AND NEW YORK.

1895

ἐγώ εἰμι ἡ ὁδὸς καὶ ἡ ἀλήθεια καὶ ἡ ζωή.
St John xiv. 6.

ἐν αὐτῷ ζῶμεν καὶ κινούμεθα καὶ ἐσμέν.
Acts xvii. 28.

First Edition 1892. Second 1895.

CHAPTER I.

THE PROBLEMS OF LIFE.

CHAPTER II.

THE DUTY AND NECESSITY OF DEALING WITH THE PROBLEMS OF LIFE.

CHAPTER III.

THE CONDITIONS UNDER WHICH A SOLUTION OF THE PROBLEMS OF LIFE MUST BE SOUGHT.

CHAPTER IV.

THE WORK OF THE PRÆ-CHRISTIAN NATIONS TOWARDS THE SOLUTION OF THE PROBLEMS OF LIFE.

CHAPTER V.

PRÆ-CHRISTIAN SOLUTIONS OF THE PROBLEMS OF BEING.

CHAPTER VI.

PRESUPPOSITIONS OF THE CHRISTIAN SOLUTION.

CHAPTER VII.

"SIGNS" AS A VEHICLE OF REVELATION.

CHAPTER VIII.

CHARACTERISTICS OF THE CHRISTIAN SOLUTION: CHRISTIANITY ABSOLUTE.

CHAPTER IX.

CHARACTERISTICS OF CHRISTIANITY: CHRISTIANITY HISTORICAL.

226896426655686969566966556666666666666666

Contents.   XV

CHAPTER X.

THE VERIFICATION OF THE CHRISTIAN SOLUTION OF THE PROBLEMS OF LIFE.

PREFACE.

THE following Chapters give the substance of Lectures which I gave from time to time (to small classes of students) during the twenty years of my work at Cambridge. The thoughts which they contain have been constantly tested in private discussion, and I have found in them guidance and support in looking at the spectacle of the world—of man and of nature—full as it is of sufferings and sorrows and failures. No one can feel more keenly than I do how fragmentary and imperfect is the expression of facts and truths which I have pondered long[1]. At least I have

---

[1] It was my intention to have added notes on the Modes and Epochs of Revelation, on the characteristics of Judaism, on the sacred Books of præ-Christian religions and on the Historical Development of Christian Doctrine, for which I have collected materials; but it is now hardly likely that I shall be able to bring the materials into a proper shape, and those who are interested in the lines of study which I have indicated will naturally seek to supply what is wanting in this respect from other sources.

endeavoured to weigh my words, and to try them again and again by the test of fresh experience. My desire has been to encourage patient reflection, to suggest lines of inquiry, to indicate necessary limits to knowledge, and not to convey formulas or ready-made arguments. Thoughts cannot be transferred: they must be appropriated.

Charged myself with the heavy responsibility of teaching, I have had constantly before me the trials, the dangers, the hopes, of teachers. The world is not clear or intelligible. If we are to deliver our message as Christians we must face the riddles of life and consider how others have faced them. So only shall we come to learn the meaning and resources of our Faith, in which we have that on which, as I believe, we can reasonably rest the whole burden of the past, the present and the future.

To some I shall necessarily appear to speak too doubtfully on questions of great moment, and to others too confidently. The relative value of different lines of thought will be variously estimated by different minds. Nothing however has been set down which does not seem to require some consideration. Not by one way but by many must we strive to reach the fulness of truth.

Every argument involves some assumptions; and I have pointed out distinctly what the Christian teacher assumes, and how far his assumptions are justified by the manifold experience of life. I have also ventured to use experience in confirmation of the Gospel which he proclaims. In spite of the objections which are used against the argument, I cannot but hold that human desire includes potentially the promise of satisfaction. The question is not, of course, of personal arbitrary or chance desires, but of those which answer to our constitution, and which have found the widest and most spontaneous expression. To think otherwise is to condemn the whole course of things as false. And if, as we assume, it answers to the will of GOD, that cannot be.

In this respect we may justly lay stress on the personal effort to grow better and on the confident expectation of general progress, in spite of numberless disappointments and delays. So through this unconquerable persistence of effort, failure becomes 'a triumph's evidence for the 'fulness of the days.'

In other words we 'walk by faith' in the face of riddles which remain to the last unanswered. Nor is there any ground for discontent at this condition of life. It not unfrequently happens that the clear perception that a difficulty is at present irremovable suggests a reasonable hope of fuller light hereafter. And though it may be

possible to put many questions aside, life is pro-
portionately impoverished if we do so.

If indeed we consider the nature of the conclusions which we form, it will appear that two
classes alone are for us absolutely valid; the
deductions which are made from the fundamental
conceptions of succession and space, and the deductions as to the operation of forces assumed to
be constant under conditions assumed to be perfectly known. As soon as we enter on the world
without and act, we enter on the unseen and the
unknown, and Faith is required to sustain and
extend thought.

But while this is so, there can be no opposition between Reason and Faith. If Reason is
the energy of the sum of man's highest powers—
of his true self—then Faith is the highest energy
of Reason. And it is most significant that the
popular antithesis of Reason and Faith finds no
place in Scripture. In Scripture the opposite to
Faith is Sight.

So it is that partial theories of life can be
formed which are logically unassailable. It is
possible to maintain with the great Hindu philosophers that there is but one existence and that
an existence purely spiritual, unchanged and
unchangeable, and that all else is a delusive
phantom. It is possible to maintain on the other

hand, that all of which we can ever be cognisant is purely material, subject to constant and inevitable change, and that all else is a mere abstraction. Both positions are beyond successful logical attack; but both are hopelessly at variance with the universal instinct and conduct of men. Men live as bound by their very nature to recognise both the reality of the outer world on the one hand, and their personal responsibility on the other. Such is the ultimate issue to which we are brought as living men; and Christianity enters at once into the fulness of life, and deals with it as men have found it to be.

For no Christian doctrine is purely speculative. No opinion as to facts of the world if vitally apprehended can fail to influence conduct, least of all the message of the Gospel. The Incarnation binds all action, all experience, all creation to GOD; and supplies at once the motive and the power of service.

In this sense the final test of the truth and the permanence of the Gospel is life, through the power of good which the Gospel exercises in every region of human thought and conduct perfectly in itself, though the use of its resources is marred by man's imperfection. We find in the lower interests of life that the best results come from action in conformity with the truth of things: are we to suppose that in the highest the law fails? and that the best results come from the false?

But it may be said that we have no right to infer the truth of a doctrine from its utility: that many beliefs have been morally useful which certainly were not true. Yet here a distinction must be made. They were effective because they were not wholly false: they were effective in virtue of the truth which they inadequately embodied. And the absolute uniqueness of Christianity lies in this that its capacity for good is universal and in itself without alloy. It has been proved to avail for all circumstances, for all races, for all times.

For Christianity offers in a real human life the thoughts by which other religions live. Nature herself does not give an answer to the riddles which she proposes; but the whole life of men points to the answer which Christianity has given. All earlier history leads up to the Incarnation: all later history has contributed to the interpretation of it. The Divine destiny of Creation and the variety of outward things: the conflict of good and evil: the responsibility of the individual and the unity of the race: the incomprehensible majesty of GOD and His infinite love: these truths, which found fragmentary expression in præ-Christian religions, are set before us in the Person and Work of the Lord, in His Birth and

Passion and Resurrection and Ascension, so that
all mysteries are brought together and reconciled
in one mystery. In the Lord Jesus Christ, One
Person, we see all things summed up, man,
humanity, creation, in the last issue of life, and
united to GOD.

Christianity is in life and through life. It is
not an abstract system but a vital power, active
through an organised body. It can never be said
that the interpretation of the Gospel is final.
For while it is absolute in its essence so that
nothing can be added to the revelation which it
includes, it is relative so far as the human apprehension of it at any time is concerned. The facts
are unchangeable but the interpretation of the
facts is progressive. Post-Christian history answers to præ-Christian history. In the latter a
Divine Covenant led up little by little to a
Divine Presence in humility. That Divine Presence itself leads up through the manifold discipline of the Church, so we believe, to a future
Divine Presence in glory. The Ascension was
the occasion of the promise of the Return.

There cannot be, I have said, any new revelation. All that we can need or know lies in the
Incarnation. But the meaning of that revelation
which has been made once for all can itself be
revealed with greater completeness. In this

sense many signs seem to shew that we are standing now on the verge of a great epoch of revelation. But however this may be, let our attitude at any rate be that of those who know that every lesson of nature and of life must illuminate the Truth which embraces the whole fulness of existence. We dishonour our Faith by anxious impatience and by jealous reservation. We believe that GOD *appointed Him heir of all things through Whom He also made the world—* the ages, time with all its contents (Hebr. i. 2). St Paul says to us, as to the Corinthians vexed and distracted by rival schools: *All things are yours: whether Paul or Apollos or Cephas or the world or life or death or things present or things to come; all are yours; and ye are Christ's; and Christ is GOD's* (1 Cor. iii. 22 f.).

B. F. D.

ROBIN HOOD'S BAY.
Sept. 13th, 1892.

NOTICE TO SECOND EDITION.

THIS edition is, with the exception of a few verbal corrections, a reprint of the former one. If other work had allowed me, I should have been glad to develop some thoughts in the essay more fully, but, even as they are presented, they will, I believe, suggest the reflections which I desired to convey, to all readers who are not (to borrow a characteristic phrase of Bishop Butler's) 'satisfied with seeing what is said, without going 'any farther.' The truths which we hold are worth to us just what they cost us and no more.

B. F. D.

AUCKLAND CASTLE,
BISHOP AUCKLAND.
Jan. 22nd, 1895.

CHAPTER I.

A RELIGION can only be understood when it is studied in relation to the facts, and the circumstances, and the experience, with which it corresponds. This is true of all religions and in the largest sense it is true of Christianity. Christianity, of which Christian Doctrine is the intellectual expression, is, like every other religion, an answer to questions which are necessarily suggested by human life. It does not introduce fresh mysteries into the world: it meets mysteries which already exist. It has been however a natural consequence of the fact that Christian Doctrine in one form or other has permeated Western civilisation and thought for many centuries, that the mysteries which belong to existence, so far as it falls within our knowledge, are commonly referred to the Christian view of existence, as if they had no independent place in human life. We first meet with them in the presentation of the Christian Faith, and we

W. G. L.   1

conclude hastily that they belong to it in some
peculiar sense.   In order therefore that we may
see clearly what Christian Doctrine really is, what
it brings that is novel either of darkness or of
light to the whole conception of being, we must
endeavour to gain some notion of the actual
circumstances in which we find ourselves, of the
problems which our condition inevitably proposes
to us, of the imperious impulses which drive us to
seek some solution of them, of the solutions which
have been formed independently during the præ-
Christian growth of humanity, before we can
rightly appreciate the characteristics of the
Christian solution.

I assume at the outset as a clear result of
personal and social experience, of the main teaching of the life of the individual and of the life of
humanity, that as men we are so constituted as
to recognise three final existences which sum up
for us all being, self, the world, and GOD ; or, to
put the thought in another form, that we are so
constituted as to recognise in that which is without us, 'the not ourselves,' something which corresponds in a certain sense to the 'body' and
'soul' which we recognise in our own being, a
'material' order and a force controlling it.

We become first conscious of the reality of

these existences through experience, through life.
And it is through experience, which we are able
to interpret, that we discern more of their nature.
The process is necessarily slow. It is only by
degrees that we learn to interpret severally the
simplest impressions of sense, the position (for
example) and the movements of objects in space;
and it is reasonable to expect that it will be
more difficult to gain a general interpretation of
the many phenomena which tend to give precision and completeness to the master thoughts
of our whole nature.

So in fact it has been and is both with the
individual and with the race. We have each of us
in the course of our own growth, and we can see
that the same is true of nations, shaped gradually
the conceptions of self, the world, and GOD, which
we now have. In this there has been nothing
arbitrary, nothing accidental. In the largest
sense we have taken 'living' as our guide in the
process, so far as it has been consciously pursued.
In part however it has been accomplished silently,
'naturally,' as we say, by a kind of moral growth.
At the same time we start on our individual
course from different points in the line of the
great inquiry. The accumulated experience of
the past is to a certain extent the inheritance
of each succeeding generation, but this wealth of

experience on which we now enter must be vitally appropriated in order that it may become effective. And it cannot be too often repeated that neither knowledge nor feeling is an end for man; we seek to know more truly and to feel more justly that we may fulfil our part in life with more perfect service.

Questioning then my own experience, and interpreting, so far as I am able, the life of others, as it falls under my observation, I hold that the assumption which I have made, that as men we necessarily recognise these three existences, self, the world, and GOD, is fully justified. The conviction rests ultimately on my personal consciousness; but, as far as I can see, my fellow-men act under the influence of the ideas which I distinguish by these names. At the same time the names are used with a wide range of meaning, and it is necessary to mark somewhat more exactly the sense in which I take them as expressing for man the final elements of being.

I am conscious of 'self.' I feel—I know, that is, immediately with the most certain assurance which I can realise—that I am something more than a collection of present sensations or thoughts. I feel that there is a past which is individually

my own, and that there will be a future, long or
short, which will be mine. I feel that there is
an inalienable continuity in a limited series of
experiences which belongs to me alone. And I
carry on the anticipation of this essential permanence of the 'I' beyond the region in which
experience can work. All around me act, as far
as I can judge, under the influence of the same
convictions. Looking without I observe that
men, to speak generally, are filled with anxiety
for their posthumous reputation; and that they
are scrupulously reverent of the dead.

I am conscious also of 'the world.' I feel,
that is, that there is outside me something finite
by which I am affected in various ways. I feel,
however difficult it may be for me to determine
the relation between my perceptions of things
and the things themselves, that my perceptions
are not originated, though they are conditioned
by my individual 'self.' I feel that my present
personal life is inconceivable without the full
recognition of the medium in which it is passed
and by which it is modified.

I am conscious in the third place of GOD.
It is not necessary for me to inquire here into
the origin of the conception. I feel that the

conception being present corresponds with what I
observe within and without. I feel, that is, that
beside the 'self' and 'the world' in which the
'self' moves, both of which are changeable and
transitory, there is That which is absolutely One
and Eternal. Each man is for himself the centre
of unity from moment to moment, but I feel that
this fleeting image of unity must answer to a
reality in which all being 'is and moves.' I feel
moreover that all that is noblest in men, all by
which they are capable of striving after the good
and the beautiful and the true, all by which
they are bound one to another, must find its
archetype in this One Eternal.

And yet more than this, when I look without,
I feel that the order which we regard gives rise
to ideas of purpose and progress which, being
what we are, we refer, under the imagery of our
own finite experience, to the action of a wise
Designer. And, last of all, the analogies of life
constrain us to think of Him as One who may
be loved and who Himself loves, while He is yet
dwelling in light unapproachable and robed in
awful majesty. I cannot think of Him as other
than Holy and Just, however feeble human words
may be to express what I dimly divine.

The consciousness of these three existences

quickened, intensified, extended, by personal and
social experience underlies, I believe, in some
degree all human thought. The consciousness
may be, and in many cases is, imperfectly defined, but it belongs to the nature of man; and
perhaps it offers the truest characterisation of
man. The final conclusion which we reach in
regard to the belief to which it witnesses more
or less clearly is that we are so made as to live
under its influence so far as it is defined. If
an objector refuses to acknowledge the reality of
any one of the three existences thus presented to
us, he occupies a position proof against all argument. A man may doubt the 'truth' of his own
sensations and of his own consciousness for the
moment or even permanently. If he does so,
and so far as he does so, he is secure against all
assaults of reasoning. But his opinions can be
brought to a practical test. If, for example, a
man apparently in the full possession of his
senses persistently says that he cannot see, and
that in fact he does not see, it is enough to
notice whether he acts as if he saw: whether his
steps are guided and his judgments formed
exactly as if he enjoyed the fulness of vision; or
whether he actually suffers the disadvantages of
blindness. In the first case, we shall feel that
there must be some misunderstanding between

us as to the nature of vision: in the second case
that, in spite of appearances, the man is defective
in that which belongs to normal humanity.

We must apply the same test to those who
make corresponding statements in regard to the
fundamental facts of morals and religion. If a
man maintains that he and his fellow-men are
automata and still dispenses praise and blame,
strives to discipline and cultivate his own powers,
watches carefully over the education of his
children: I must conclude that in spite of his
words he really believes that man is ' free,' that is,
individually responsible, no less than I do, though
he does not express his belief in the same
language. Or again if he holds the permanence
of law, and holds also that there is on the whole a
progress in the world and in humanity towards
a higher and nobler type of being and living, and
consciously and confidently accepts his part in
furthering it: then even if he says that GOD is
beyond human knowledge, I cannot but see that
he has acknowledged what I hold to be of the
essence of the idea of GOD. And so it is that
many who theoretically affirm that they are
automata, or that the world exists only in the
mind of man, or that there is no GOD, yet
shew in action that they have a more practical
belief in personal responsibility, in Nature, and

in GOD than some who do not pause to question the common Creed. Here as elsewhere we are taught to know men as they really are not by words but by experience.

We find ourselves then face to face with these ultimate elements of being and thought; and as soon as we begin to reflect upon any one of them, as soon as we begin to act, we are beset by speculative difficulties and contradictions. Each existence, as we have come to apprehend it, brings its own difficulties with it; and the difficulties of each taken by themselves are final, inexplicable. Whether we admit 'self' alone to be the one ultimate existence which we know, or recognise self and the world, or self and the world and GOD, we must bear with what patience or faith we can mysteries which are like in kind though they may differ in number. These mysteries furnish the problems with which religions deal, problems which we have now to endeavour to apprehend, problems which, as I believe, Christianity solves so far as a solution is possible, though it does not alone or primarily propose them.

i. We will take the idea of 'self' first. We have no sooner named the word than we are confronted with an overwhelming mystery. What can we say as to the *origin* of 'self'? How can we adjust in thought the relation of the child to the line from which he springs? How much do we derive directly from our parents, and where or from what source is that communicated which gives to us our individuality? We may say, and say with justice, that 'the dead rule the living,' but what are the limits of their dominion? The most absolute tyrant finds bounds set to his power somewhere. And the idea of 'self' involves separation, personality, something which is ours only. How do we obtain and justify that conception of 'our own'?

We go a step further. The germ of 'self' is given, and we watch the progress of its development. The growth of this personality is up to a certain point like the growth of a plant. The product of any particular seed is fixed within the limits of a type, while within these limits there is room for the widest variation in health, and vigour, and shape, and colour, and beauty, and fruitfulness, from the action of external influences which we can trace and measure. So it is, up to a certain point, with a man. His type of character is fixed at his birth: and at the same time there is the possibility of endless differences in the particular realisation of the type from the conditions of the environment under which it takes outward shape. It would be easy to multiply illustrations. No one who has looked patiently and reverently upon life will be inclined to underrate the influences upon a man's nature which are wholly beyond his control, influences of country and class and parentage and education and material circumstances. It is of momentous consequence for the final character of any one whether he be one of many or an only child in his first home; whether he belong to a class accustomed to rule, or to a class accustomed to labour or to serve; whether he be a Latin or a Celt or a Teuton; whether he be born in the 9th or the 19th century. We hardly realise how even a lifeless machine or a mere intellectual conception can stir human life to its inmost depths, so that a discovery made at a particular time separates by an ineffaceable partition those who came before from those who come after. The steam-engine, for example, not only increased enormously the power of material transformations, but it has also modified irrevocably the conditions of labour, that is, it has modified the conditions of the social discipline of men. Or, to take an illustration of the other class, the Copernican system has changed the whole aspect

of the universe for man, and with this the whole
influence which it exercises upon his character.
It has given the earth a new position in relation
to the stellar system which later investigations are
slowly enabling us to interpret. And the lesson
is one which we shall do well to take to heart.
For, if for a time it appeared that we had lost
something by the removal of our globe from its
central place, we are now beginning to see that the
final effect of the changed view is to ennoble our
conception alike of the world and of man's place
in it; to lead us to abandon a physical standard
in our estimate of things; to perceive a harmony
between the conditions of being realised in space
and the conditions of being realised in time;
for there is nothing irrational in supposing that
the earth occupies towards the material universe
a position corresponding to that which man
occupies with regard to the multitudinous forms
of life, which, as we observe them in geological
records, converge towards him as their crown.
The earth, that is, is brought back again to be
a true centre in a deeper sense than that of
local position. And no one probably will now
deny that the heliocentric view of our system,
passing, as it necessarily does, into some dim
conception of a still vaster order, when it is thus
considered, is more religious and, in the fullest

sense, more Scriptural than the geocentric view which it displaced.

By this signal illustration we can see how the interpretation of the same conception, as well as the introduction of a new conception, may profoundly influence the commonest and the highest thoughts of man. The same law holds good even where at present we are less able to trace its working, as in theories of creation and development, of law, and the like. Man, in a word, is dependent on that which lies outside himself socially, materially, intellectually; and the results of this dependence reach to every part of his being. He is dependent on the past, from which he draws his inheritance of manifold wealth for thought and action. He is dependent on the present, in which he finds the scene, the materials, and the conditions of his activity. He is dependent even on the future, in which he finds through hope the inspiration and support of effort which cannot bring a return within the limits of his hour of work.

Man is dependent: this is one side of the Truth. But his circumstances are the materials out of which he has to build his life with an indeterminate personal power. He is conscious of responsibility; this consciousness is indeed the essence of the idea of 'self.' Man, to state the case shortly, 'depends upon the circumstances to 'which he owes his origin and under which he 'lives, but, in the fulness of his nature, he does 'not result from them.' He acknowledges that he is responsible: there is the witness to the fact of essential freedom; he acknowledges that he fails: there is the witness to the imperfection of freedom.

It is not possible here to enter in any detail into the discussion of the nature of 'freedom,' but it is of the utmost importance that we should avoid one prevalent error about it. We must, that is, carefully distinguish freedom from the simple power of doing any thing under any circumstances. Such a power would be potential slavery. Freedom is the power to effect the *one* right thing which presents the perfect harmony of the agent and the circumstances. Freedom is positive and not neutral. It is the ability to fulfil the law of our being without let or hindrance, to do what we ought to do; and this presupposes for its perfection and permanence the absolute inability to do what is contrary to our proper nature. Thus there are two distinct elements in freedom, self-determination and right determination. Our consciousness tells us that we have freedom in the sense of self-determination, but that disturbing influences interfere with the fitness of our choice. For man in his essential nature, no less than in his actual condition, perfect freedom is the result of discipline through which right action becomes habitual and finally assured. In the last and highest form man's freedom is the conscious acceptance of that which he knows to be the will of GOD[1].

The conflict between our dependence and our freedom is felt in all its intensity when we look within. Self is one and one indivisibly; and yet popular language which expresses the common experience of men and our own personal experience constrains us to distinguish elements, so to speak, in this unity. We say popularly, to use the broadest division, that we are made up of 'mind' (soul) and 'matter' (body). Nothing, at

---

[1] Compare Aug. *in Ps.* cxv., § 6. Omnis creatura subdita Creatori est, et verissimo Domino verissimum debet famulatum, quem cum exhibet libera est, hanc accipiens a Domino gratiam ut ei non necessitate sed voluntate deserviat.

Ep. clvii. (col. 89), 7 f. Desinant ergo sic insanire, et ad hoc se intelligant habere quantum possunt liberum arbitrium, non ut superba voluntate respuant adjutorium sed ut pia voluntate invocent Dominum. Hæc enim voluntas libera tanto erit liberior quanto sanior: tanto autem sanior quanto divinæ misericordiæ gratiæque subjectior.

Cypr. *ad Don.* c. 4. Dei est inquam, Dei est omne quod possumus: inde vivimus, inde pollemus...

first seems easier than to distinguish them
sharply: and so it is that we all are inclined to
set them apart in actual existence. But if we
proceed far with the exact definition of the
difference we shall be met by difficulties analogous to those which occur in fixing the limits of
'life' and of the different types of life. These
difficulties may—and we must be prepared for
the result—prove to be insurmountable. The last
word of Truth on the subject may be, and every
word of Truth is precious to the Christian, that
for man mind and matter are both abstractions
and not independent realities.

But however little we may be able to define
the limits or explain the mutual action of mind
and matter, of body, soul, and spirit in the fuller
division of Scripture, we are conscious of rival
impulses which stir us. Our being does not move
as one harmonious whole. Just as we strive to
overcome obstacles without, we find ourselves
striving to overcome obstacles within. In both
cases alike we feel the effort: we know that it
costs us something: we acknowledge that we are
answerable for making or neglecting to make it.
Our whole life is spent in aiming at something
which we cannot reach, but no ill success absolves
us from the necessity of further labour. There is
in those whom common consent allows to be men

of the noblest type, an unending endeavour to attain to higher knowledge and purer virtue. But as far as our eyes can reach, or the experience of others can enlighten us, the best and saintliest fall far short to the last of what they believe to have been within their power. There is something in us—'a baseness in the blood'—different from weakness : an evil, a perversion in our nature. There is an actual shadow over life.

This sense of present personal failure is sharpened by the inexorable sternness of 'Nature.' 'Nature' appears to be wholly regardless of the individual. There may be mercy elsewhere, but physical laws shew none, and offer no promise that it will be found. Another rule may hold good in another order, but these, as every day teaches us with appalling emphasis, visit the sins of fathers upon the children unto the third and fourth generation, and claim from him who violates them the last farthing of the penalty. For man, so far as he has and transmits a material nature, there is no release from inevitable consequences. Yet here again a mystery,—the old mystery of Prometheus,—opens before us. Man feels his powerlessness in the face of physical forces, and yet he feels that he is greater than they. They go on and he vanishes away, but

his fellows after him undismayed reassert their
preëminence.

We carry our thoughts yet further. It is
true that a beginning seems to our reason to
imply an end, but we refuse to accept the consequence. It is true that death closes what we can
see of life, but we cannot admit that it closes life.
The conviction that 'we' shall survive that last
change remains unshaken when every argument
by which the conviction is supported gives way.
The contrast, the antagonism, between what we
can see and what we feel, our attainments and
our powers, which follows us all through our
present existence becomes most marked at the
end.

The mystery of birth is consummated in the
mystery of death. And, what is most amazing,
we cling to our belief in a life to come, while yet,
as far as we can see, Nature offers no hope
of forgiveness. The terrible law, embodied by
Æschylus, according to which evil acts propagate
in endless succession a progeny like themselves,
seems to sum up what we can learn by experience
of the retribution of evil doing. No repentance
on earth can undo the past. We cannot unmake
ourselves. And further than this, and yet more
appalling, no personal repentance or amendment

can, as far as we see, undo the evil of which we have been the occasion to others. Of all visions none can be more terrible than that of the man who looks towards a future state in which shall be realised the full and due results of this life in the way of natural sequence. For if we regard the whole matter from the side of reason we shall see that the greatest mystery of the life to come is not the prospect of unending retribution, but the possibility of blotting out the consequences of sin.

Now these mysteries of 'self' are facts. Every one knows that they are real apart from all religious belief whatever. Our origin, our growth, our independence and freedom, our constitution, our personal dignity, our destiny, offer problems which we cannot refuse to consider except at the cost of abdicating our loftiest privileges. Christianity did not introduce these problems into life; it did not even first reveal them. They are and they always will be while time is. Christianity is addressed to man and to humanity as living in the face of them. And as we come to see them more plainly we shall come to know better what Christianity is, for Christianity, as we shall see hereafter, enables us to contemplate them with certain hope.

ii. From 'self' we turn to 'the world.' This
sphere of being also is beset by mysteries which
are commonly unobserved from the fact that the
surface of things offers enough to occupy and
distract our attention.

We are, as we have seen, forced to believe
that there is an external world : yet how little
do we reflect that there is here any room for faith
where knowledge may seem to be immediate.
But no one who does pause to reflect can fail to
discern that no mystery can be greater than that
which is involved in the passage from the perceptions of things which belong to us alone to
the things themselves outside us. All that we
can say is that just as we are constituted to believe
in the continuity of our own existence, so are we
constituted to believe in the reality of an outward world corresponding to our perceptions.
We do not attempt to distinguish in any particular case the elements in the whole impression
which belong respectively to that which produces
the impression and to that which is conscious
of it. We have, so to speak, a single equation
and two unknown quantities. So it is generally,
and so it is also with regard to the several
impressions, which we receive in detail in connexion with special conditions. We do not know
enough either of ourselves or of that which is

not ourselves to enable us to assign to that which is without and that which is within their shares in the whole result. But it is no less a duty to acknowledge that the simplest of human experiences, the perception of a green leaf or of the blue sky, involves mysteries.

How, for example, can we form any notion of the world as it was before the existence of man? We cannot suppose that it existed only in relation to a being not yet formed. We cannot say that things are always perceived by GOD as man perceives them and so exist. Evidently we are met by an insoluble problem; and it is well that we should feel that the problem lies before us and that it is insoluble. It is at least a sign of the limitation of our powers in a direction where we can conceive that knowledge is possible through other faculties than those which we possess.

Here then is our primal difficulty. We have acknowledged it: our way is still beset by another. There is the mystery of a beginning, which may be taken as the type of all mysteries of finiteness. It is as impossible to conceive by a mere effort of thought that the world had a beginning as it is to conceive that it had not a beginning. We might therefore be inclined to reckon this question like the last as one wholly insoluble by reason. But light here comes from an unexpected quarter; and larger experience points to a distinct decision as far as the present order is concerned. If we pursue the interpretation of phenomena sufficiently far, we are forced to conclude that the present order has existed only for a finite time, or in other words that the present order cannot be explained on the supposition of the continuous action of forces which we can now observe, acting according to the laws which represent to us what we can observe of the characteristics of their action.

This conclusion that the world, as we know it, has existed only for a measurable time is one of the latest and perhaps most unlooked for results of physical research. The general law from which it follows is known as that of 'the dissipation of energy.' This principle is the correlative of the law of the conservation of energy which is 'the most complete expression hitherto 'obtained of the belief that all the changes of 'phenomena are but different distributions of the 'same stock of energy, the total quantity of which 'remains invariable. This energy is conserved 'but it may be dissipated. It is indestructible 'but it may cease to be available, when it cannot 'be made to do visible work.'[1] This work may be, under the conditions of our system, reduced to three kinds: the production of visible motion; the communication of heat from a hotter to a colder body; the transference of pressure in a system of constant volume from parts under great pressure to parts where the pressure is less. Now in each of these cases the doing of work is accompanied by a diminution of available energy. If, for example, visible motion is produced a certain amount of energy is lost by friction; or, in another aspect of the same case, if heat is transformed into motion, a part of the heat is forthwith diffused, and, when so diffused, it cannot afterwards be made effective to produce action. This diffusion therefore and generally this diminution of available energy can only have been continued for a limited time, for otherwise the end of a dead equilibrium would have been already reached.

'We have,' in other words, 'an irreversible 'process always going on, at a greater or less rate, 'in the universe. If therefore there was ever 'an instant at which the whole energy of the 'universe was available energy, that instant must 'have been the very first instant at which the uni-'verse began to exist. If there ever shall come a 'time at which the whole energy of the universe

[1] Prof. Clerk Maxwell, in *Nature*, IX. pp. 198 ff.

'has become unavailable, the history of the uni-
'verse will then have reached its close. During
'the whole intervening period the available energy
'has been diminishing and the unavailable in-
'creasing by a process as irresistible and as irre-
'versible as Time itself. The duration of the
'universe according to the present order of
'things is therefore essentially finite both *a parte*
'*ante* and *a parte post.*'[1]

In other words the assumed permanence of
the existing laws of matter involves the consequence that the universe had a beginning within
a measurable time; and if it be said that we have
no right to assume the uniform action in the past
of the laws which hold good now, that is to con-
cede at once what is for us equivalent to a
creative act.

The general law, which points to a historical beginning of the present order, finds
expression in a particular case which is of great
interest. The formulæ which represent the observed laws of the conduction of heat force us to
take account at some point in the past of a
creative act, that is of a discontinuity in the
present order of phenomena. According to these
formulæ it is possible to foresee the thermal

[1] Prof. Clerk Maxwell, in *Nature*, IX. p. 200.

condition of any number of bodies at any future time so long as thermal action only takes place between them. If we go back, the same process may be reversed for a certain distance and the condition of the bodies may be referred to an earlier and continuous action of the same kind. But at last a limit is reached at which the condition of the bodies can no longer be explained in the same way. At this point then some change must have taken place in the relation of the bodies which marked essentially a fresh beginning.

Again I will use the words of a master to describe the fact:

'The irreversible character of this process '[the dissipation of energy] is strikingly embodied 'in Fourier's theory of the conduction of heat, 'where the formulæ themselves indicate a possi-'ble solution of all positive values of the time 'which continually tends to a uniform diffusion of 'heat. But if we attempt to ascend the stream 'of time by giving to its symbol continually 'diminishing values, we are led up to a state of 'things in which the formula has what is called a 'critical value; and if we inquire into the state of 'things the instant before, we find that the 'formula becomes absurd. We thus arrive at 'the conception of a state of things which cannot 'be conceived as the physical result of a previous 'state of things, and we find that this critical 'condition actually existed at an epoch not in the 'utmost depths of a past eternity but separated 'from the present time by a finite interval.'[1]

Thus the principle of the dissipation of energy suggests distinctly both a beginning and an end of the present order. It suggests also some creative action, so far at least as to make it clear that the laws which we can trace now will not allow us to suppose that the order which they express has existed for ever. Physicists have gone yet farther. If matter is pursued to its ultimate form, we find at last, according to the most competent judgment, molecules incapable of subdivision without change of substance, which are absolutely similar for each substance. A molecule of hydrogen, for example, has exactly the same weight, the same period of vibration, the same properties in every respect, whether it be found in the Earth or in the Sun or in Sirius. The relations of the parts and movements of the planetary systems may and do change, but these molecules—'the foundation stones of the material universe—remain unbroken and unworn.' 'No theory of evolution can be

[1] Clerk Maxwell, Address at Brit. Assoc., Liverpool, Sept. 1870. (*Nature*, II. pp. 421 f.)

'formed to account for the similarity of mole-
'cules, for evolution necessarily implies continuous
'change, and the molecule is incapable of growth
'or decay, of generation or destruction. None of
'the processes of Nature, since the time when
'Nature began, have produced the slightest dif-
'ference in the properties of any molecule. We
'are therefore unable to ascribe either the exist-
'ence of the molecules or the identity of their
'properties to the operation of any of the causes
'which we call natural....The exact quality of
'each molecule...precludes the idea of its being
'eternal and self-existent.'[1] We cannot, in other
words, represent to ourselves the ground of this
final and immutable similarity in any other way
than as a result of a definite creative will.

So much at least is clear, that the mystery of
creation is not introduced by religion.   It is
forced upon us by the world itself, if we look
steadily upon the world.   And no mystery can
be greater than this inevitable mystery.

Again : if we turn from the conception of becoming to that of being, from creation to orderly
existence, we find ourselves confronted with· new

[1] *Nature*, VIII. p. 441. (Molecules, a Lecture delivered at
Bradford, 1873, by J. Clerk Maxwell. Compare Introductory
Lecture on Experimental Physics, pp. 21 ff.)

difficulties. The idea of law as applied to the succession of external phenomena rests simply upon faith. We extend to the world, with necessary modifications, the idea of persistence which underlies the consciousness of 'self.' The conception of uniform repetition, of the permanence of that which is, is supplied by us from within to the results of observation. We are so constituted as to conclude with more or less confidence from a certain number of uninterrupted repetitions, that the series will continue. We are so constituted as to extend this form of conclusion boldly even where the result depends upon the combination of many conditions which may severally fail of fulfilment. And in affirming that the succession in any case will be uniform, we do not simply affirm that the same antecedents will produce the same consequents—the opposite of which is inconceivable—but, which is a very different thing, that like antecedents will produce like consequents, and that in any particular case, we know all the antecedents, and know them fully, of which we cannot possibly be sure. Absolute accuracy in concrete things is unattainable. In the present order of things no antecedent can be the same in two cases. Nothing can actually recur. Every phenomenon is in its completeness unique. We may indeed be sure that *if* the force of gravitation continues to act ten days hence as it has acted during all past experience, and *if* our formulæ express adequately all the conditions of its action, and *if* no other force, acting, it may be, periodically, shall interfere, then the sun will rise at the time to which we look forward. But each one of these suppositions is justified by belief and not by knowledge. The belief becomes confirmed day by day as that which was future becomes past. But the past in itself can give us no knowledge of the future. With regard to that we can to the end only have a belief; so that Faith lies at the basis of our confidence in natural law.

As we reflect, difficulties still thicken round us. What we call 'a law' describes in its simplest form the general relation of phenomena so far as we have observed them. Practically, from the very nature of the case, we are able only to see a little, and that little for a little time; but for purposes of reasoning we assume that what we observe will be permanent, and inasmuch as the conditions and the field of our observation do not vary greatly, experience may justify the assumption as far as it goes, though still the assumption may be false; just as it is easy to imagine a circle so large that a small arc might not be distinguishable from a straight line by any measurements which we could make. And further if we are at liberty to assume that what we call ' laws ' are uniform for us and for the whole range of our possible experience, still they finally explain nothing. A ' law ' has no virtue to shew its own constitution or beginning. A law can reveal nothing of the absolute nature of that which works according to it. So far from doing this, laws constrain us to ask more importunately, as we grow more sensible of their simplicity, how we can conceive of their origin? how we can conceive of that—however we call it—which they present to us in action? A law does not dispense with these questions but sharpens and reiterates them. If we follow out intently the movements of bodies and their vital transformations we shall look more intently than other men to that which binds phenomena together and guides present human life.

The idea of law leads directly to that of harmony. And at all times men have been profoundly impressed by the signs of a magnificent unity in the world. They have seemed to themselves to see these in every wide view of the material universe and of the general course and conditions of life. From age to age, as

knowledge has widened, it has appeared to great
teachers to be more and more clear that there has
been a progress in the physical world and in the
moral world. The rapidity and confidence, for
example, with which the theory of 'development'
has been welcomed within our own time, a theory
which has found acceptance out of all proportion
to the direct value of the evidence by which it is
supported, witness to the power of this tendency
in man's interpretation of the phenomena of life.
We do not at present inquire whether these signs
of progress find their fulfilment. It is enough
that they should commonly be held to be legible.
The mystery of an end, far-off as it may be,
towards which the universe is moving, crowns
the mystery of creation and the mystery of law.

But side by side with the signs of an under-
lying or unattained unity in the world, out of
which it appears to rise or towards which it
appears to move, when it is regarded in its broad
extent, there are also countless losses, interrup-
tions, conflicts in the visible condition of things.
To one observer the present spectacle of the races
of men becomes a vision of despair, to another a
preparation for a natural millennium. But whether
our eyes are fixed on the present or on the future
the actual discord is often enough to banish the

thought of the promised harmony. It is not necessary to discuss in detail the character of these conflicting indications of truth and falsehood, of beauty and ugliness, goodness and cruelty, or how far the failure or sacrifice of fragments may be made to subserve to the well-being of the whole. Storms, earthquakes, eruptions on the one side, wars and passions on the other, proclaim the broad lesson of suffering and imperfection in the world, so far as our observation reaches, with alarming vividness. The very fact that some speculators in all ages have affirmed that the only adequate explanation of the origin of the present state of things is to be found in the antagonism of two rival powers wrought out on earth, is sufficient to shew the reality of this struggle between good and evil. However we may account for the beginning or for the continuance of it, the struggle is going on. This mystery again is one from which there is no escape.

The struggle is going on without us and within us, in the world and in ourselves, and we partake in the whole struggle. This consideration brings into light a new mystery. That which has been called 'the pathetic fallacy' reveals, as I believe, one of the profoundest truths of being.

There is a life running through all creation in
which we share. We severally think with a mind
which is more or less in harmony with a universal
mind. It is more than a mere metaphor to say
that we have sympathy with Nature and Nature
with us. And if we are startled to find that the
action of the mind is connected with certain definite changes of matter as physiologists have established, we must remember that the reasonable
conclusion from this fact is not that the mind is
material, in the sense of being corruptible and
transitory, but that matter is spiritual. For it
shews that the one force exerted through matter
of which we are conscious is such.

And what must be said of the future?
What indications are there of the issue of this
conflict which reaches through all being and all
life? Must we suppose that things move on in a
uniform course? or that they revolve in cycles?
There is at least no ground in the being of things
themselves to expect a progress, an advance from
good to better, in nature or in history. The
'survival of the fittest' through conflict, in respect
of the conditions of present physical existence, by
no means assures us of the survival of the fittest
absolutely, in respect of the highest capacities of
human nature. If we find that we cling to the

belief that the world does so advance, then this
persistency of faith can only be due to the conviction that there is a true moral government
of the universe : that the evil is something which
does not belong to the essence of creation and is
therefore separable from it : that the contest here
is not a war between rival powers, but a rebellion
of a subject against his lord.

iii. In this way the world adds its mysteries to the sum of the dark problems of life,
the mysteries of man's perception of the world,
of creation, of law, of that which acts by law,
of conflict, of unity, of sympathy, of progress.
They lie before us, whether we regard them or
not; and consciously or unconsciously we all deal
with them.   Nor is this all.   They lead us up at
last to other mysteries, the last mysteries of being
on which I propose to touch, the mysteries which
are involved in the idea of GOD.   This idea is, I
have assumed, natural to man, and necessarily
called out into some form of distinctness just as
the other ideas of 'self' and 'the world.'   But
difficulties begin as soon as we attempt to set
our thoughts upon it in order.

If we try to establish by argument the
existence of a Being Whom we may reverence

and love, our intellectual proofs break down. The 'proofs' which are derived from the supposed necessity that something must remain fixed in the midst of change, or that a real being must correspond to the highest thought of man, if they are pressed to their last consequences, issue in pantheism. The 'proofs' again which are derived from the observation of design, of the adaptation of means to an end, or from the dictates of conscience, make man and man's ways of thinking measures of all being in a manner which cannot be justified. Nor would they lead to an adequate conclusion. The Being to which they guide us is less than the Being for Whom we look and in Whom we trust. Such arguments are fitted to bring into greater distinctness that knowledge of GOD, which man is born to pursue, to quicken and to illustrate his search for it, to shew the correspondence of the higher idea of GOD which he shapes with the suggestions and signs of nature and action and thought. But they have no final or absolute validity. We can know that only which falls *within* the range of our minds.

We abandon then, it may be, all attempts to prove by reason what we find to be true in experience, and simply strive to give reality to the idea which we have. As we do so, we are at

3—2

once baffled by the conception of the 'personality' of GOD. For us 'personality' is expressed by and is the expression of limitation. How can we extend this notion to an Infinite Being? and, if this is impossible, how then can we supply in any other way that which shall give to the idea the definiteness which we long for?

Or we may approach the difficulty from another side. Just as 'personality' corresponds with our human notion of the Being of GOD; so prayer corresponds with our notion of the action of GOD. Prayer is a universal instinct. But when we come to analyse what we suppose to be the action of prayer addressed to GOD, it seems to involve the movement of the infinite by the finite. The instinct remains but we cannot reconcile the contradiction which it brings out. It represents to us in the most impressive shape the mystery which lies in the coexistence of the finite and the infinite.

The question of prayer carries us on to consider the relation of GOD not only to ourselves but also to the world. Does the observed uniformity of law embody the present will of GOD acting so to speak from moment to moment? or must we suppose that 'all creation was one act at once,'

and that the succession of phenomena in our
experience is a consequence of the weakness of
our powers as we decipher the Divine thought?
The mere effort to ponder the questions is
sufficient to shew the irrelevance of much of the
popular reasoning about 'miracles.' The 'law'
under which we arrange our observations has no
independent force. Ordinary and exceptional
phenomena equally reveal the action of GOD, and
we can have no certain assurance that we have
at any time learnt all the ways of His working.

Such considerations disclose the undiscover-
able vastness of the order in which we are set;
and through, or at least according to, which we
must learn whatever the imperfection of our
powers allows us to learn of GOD. The immediate
contemplation of nature is overwhelming; and
the actual history of human opinion brings no
assistance towards the solution of the mystery of
the relation of GOD to the world and to ourselves.
If we fix our thoughts on the præ-Christian period
it will be seen that the religious history of men,
whether Jews or Heathen, is the history of the
gradual withdrawal of GOD from the world. In
the first ages, as in the childhood of the race or
in our own childhood, GOD seemed to be very near
to men and easily to be approached. So it is

written in the history of the Old Testament.
The Patriarchs communed with GOD and made
covenants with Him. Little by little He was
withdrawn and shrouded in more awful majesty.
His voice alone was heard through the Prophets.
At last His name was left unspoken. An elabo-
rate and splendid ritual, while it brought to some
intelligible signs of spiritual promises, satisfied
the desires of others; and the hope of a further
revelation of His will became the mark of a sect
in the chosen people.

The same kind of change passed over the
creeds of the Gentile nations. At the dawn of
history traditions that the gods had walked
among men were still current. Afterwards local
and limited deities kept alive the familiar sense
of a divine presence. Then came the dissolving
power of speculation. The old faith was degraded
in each case into a lifeless superstition: the new
faith vainly aspired to deify a mere phantom of
thought. At the best the abstract notion of a
Providence was suggested to those who had
thirsted for a living GOD; or some form of Pantheism offered to the believer union with the
object of his belief, while it took from him every
thing to which he could direct his affections.

Apart from revelation—apart from the final

revelation in Christ—this must, as it appears, be
the tragic course of human experience both in the
society and in the individual life.   As we come
to apprehend more clearly what we are and what
GOD in Himself must be, the interval between
the creature and the Creator opens out in its
infinite depth.   Reason fails and then feeling.
But the craving for GOD remains unsatisfied and
unextinguished.   This craving is as much a fact
of nature as any other fact; and, even when the
reality seems to be farthest off, man still longs for
One Who is Eternal, and One Whom he can love.

We can now see some of the mysteries which
life necessarily carries with it.   If we have advanced so far in our education as to look calmly
upon the conditions of our being we shall find
that such questions as these are irresistibly borne
in upon us: How do we regard 'self' in relation
to its origin and to its development?   What
account do we take in our estimate of humanity
of the necessary dependence of man upon circumstances?   How do we reconcile this dependence
with the sense of responsibility?   What explanation can we give of our restless striving after an
unattainable ideal? of our invincible self-assertion
in the face of the material forces of nature? of
our confident anticipations of life beyond death?

Or again: what is the beginning, and support
and end of the world? How can we harmonise
the magnificent promises of order and unity with
the existence of conflict and waste? How do we
explain that

> sense sublime
> Of something far more deeply interfused,
> Whose dwelling is the light of setting suns
> And the round ocean, and the living air
> And the blue sky, and in the mind of man.

With what hope or aspiration do we look forward to a consummation of things wherein their
original destiny shall be reconciled with their
abiding condition?

Or yet again: How do we adjust our idea of
GOD to the conditions of our own existence and
to the phenomena of the world? How do we
retain it in all its intensity in spite of the age-
long experience which seems to remove GOD
farther from us?

How, in a word, can we gain permanence for
the foundation of religious faith? How can
our Creed be invested with that vitality of form
which shall grow with all the growth of men and
mankind? Truth, if it is to affect our whole life
which is one and indivisible, must be expressed
for us in a Fact. Theology based upon external
or internal Nature, upon observation or con-

sciousness, is unstable and inadequate to our
wants. It brings no decisive interpretation to
conflicting phenomena. Theology based upon
isolated communications of the Divine will must
be relative to special circumstances. We reach
out therefore to a real and abiding union of GOD
and man, as real as that which Pantheism establishes between the fragment and the whole: as
personal as that which the simplest faith has
believed to exist between the worshipper and
the object of his adoration. And we do so with
confidence because we trust that the system of
the world answers to Truth, and that the desire
of the race is, in its highest form as in each
partial form, a promise of fulfilment.

To ask such questions is to propose problems of the greatest difficulty. It requires a
serious effort even to seize their scope. Some
indeed may feel impatient that they should be
raised for discussion. And I gladly acknowledge
that the power of the Christian life is for the most
part independent of speculative inquiries. Yet
there is an office of the thinker and the teacher.
Each age offers its characteristic riddles; and it
is by man's endeavour to solve these as they
come that that fuller apprehension of the Truth
is reached through which nobler action becomes

more widely possible. If then we approach the spiritual problems of our own age, not in any conceit of intellectual superiority, but as accepting a grave duty and using an opportunity of service, we may reasonably look for some new blessing. To face them, to ponder them reverently, is to feel the glory which belongs to the nature of man unfallen: to have the assurance of solving them, so far as a solution is required for the guidance and inspiration of life, is to know the gift of GOD which is brought to us by the Gospel of the Resurrection.

CHAPTER II.

FROM what has been already said it must be
sufficiently clear that life is beset by mysteries
and to strive to banish these mysteries from
thought is to impoverish our whole existence.
They form the solemn background of all experience; and the exclusion of every religious theory
from our view of life will not in fact make life
plain and intelligible. On the contrary the fuller
apprehension of the character of the mysteries
which necessarily attend our being, impels us
more forcibly to seek for some solution of the
practical problems which they present, for such a
solution as religion claims to bring. What shall
we say of the complex and disordered constitution
of man, of the issues of sin, of the confident expectation with which we look forward to a life after

death? What shall we say of the relation of the individual to the race and to the world in which he is placed? What shall we say of the possibility of a knowledge of GOD?

No questions can be asked which have a more momentous significance than these, and all experience shews the importunate eagerness with which men, in proportion as they have grown in knowledge, have sought answers to them. The history of metaphysics is a continuous witness to the irresistible attraction which they have exercised upon the most profound thinkers; and whatever opinion may be entertained as to the purely metaphysical answers which have been rendered to them, the fact that such answers have found a welcome in all ages indicates the direction of human desire. This desire embodies itself in some shape or other by what appears to be a necessity of our nature; and even those students who have endeavoured to confine themselves to physical research—who have sought to obtain an understanding of the world from without and not from within—have unconsciously extended their theories beyond their assumed limits. It cannot be otherwise. For these final problems, which lie at the root of Christian Doctrine, meet us in whichever direction we turn. They stand in the closest relation to life. They must be dealt with in some way or other. The kind of treatment which they receive cannot but have an important bearing upon conduct. They correspond with the development of one side of man's multiform nature. The problems, in other words, are unavoidable: they are practical: they are educational. The consideration of them enters into all thought: it has a power to direct and stimulate action: it is effective in moulding character.

i. The problems are unavoidable. We cannot, that is, escape from the necessity of dealing with the questions suggested by a consideration of these final existences, self, the world, GOD; and, this being so, the duty of investigating them is laid upon those for whom it is possible, because, with or without reflection, we must accept and act upon some decision concerning them. This is unquestionable. Every action on our part involves a judgment of some kind or other upon controversies which have been maintained and are still maintained as to our responsibility, our powers, our destiny.

The theory which sways our conduct, whether we know it or not, has taken shape with our own growth and become in a true sense part of ourselves. It may be simply the result of the

moral atmosphere which we breathe: it may be
the fruit of sustained and arduous effort. But in
either case the influence of the theory of life
which we hold implicitly or avowedly is real and
it is effective. However indifferent we may be to
independent speculation, the average opinion, if
the phrase may be used, which we share represents the issues of long and vehement controversies.
It expresses fairly, if on a low level, what has been
ascertained in the past from the interpretation of
consciousness in the light of history—including all
that is contained in the Bible—as to our freedom,
and as to our relation to the finite and the infinite.
And this popular Creed is never stationary. The
inner and outer boundaries of knowledge are
ever advanced without cessation or break. It is
as true in metaphysics as it is in physics that the
goal of yesterday is the starting-post of to-day,
though the repetition of identical terms in the
former case may suggest the simple recurrence of
ideas. But no such literal recurrence is possible.
Each fresh discovery as to the relations of the complex elements which go to form our personality; or
as to the limits of variation to which our powers
and faculties are open under given circumstances;
or as to the dependence of thought upon external
conditions; or as to the most general formulae
under which the phenomena of being can be

grouped; or as to the ultimate connexion and unity of life: must sooner or later pass into the universal heritage of men; and when the results of science thus become, as they do become, with more or less delay, an element in the circumstances under which men think and move, they are continuously effective as moral forces. The incorporation of such physical and historical and moral discoveries or revelations, as we may prefer to call them, into the common Creed, must take place, but it may take place in different ways, silently so that indifferent spectators are unaware of the change which is going on about them, or by a sharp crisis of conflict which shakes faith to its foundations. The true Theologian therefore will look with vigilant sympathy in every direction for each fragment which can be added to his treasure. Those who are called upon to teach the study of Theology will acknowledge that it is their office to prepare the way for the admission of new aspects of Truth into the current estimate of life, and to provide against the misconceptions of impatient controversy, and the waste of sectarianism. And those students of Theology who have the opportunity will strive from the first and with glad willingness to assimilate the acquisitions of inquiry. In some way or other both teacher and student must acknowledge in time the power

of the new influences. It is only left for them
to choose whether they will do so with ready fore-
sight, or simply under that blind pressure which is
disastrous in proportion as it is alarming.

ii. This is the choice which lies before us;
and the importance of the choice is at once apprehended in its true extent, if we observe that these
ultimate problems of being, both in their most
general form and in their details, carry with them
direct practical consequences. All experience goes
to shew that conduct in the long run corresponds
with belief. The public opinion which prevails in
a nation or a class is more powerful to repress and
to urge than legal sanctions of punishment and
reward. The coercion of law is effective only so
far as the law embodies a dominant opinion; and,
as a natural corollary, law is actually a little
behind popular opinion. But a dominant opinion
sooner or later finds expression in law by the
enactment of restrictions or by the removal of
them.   .

This unquestionable principle carries with it
momentous consequences. If it could be established that man's actions are the necessary result
of his individual constitution and his circumstances, in such a sense that he has no real control
over them, morality would be at an end. If it

could be shewn that such a crisis as death makes
it inconceivable that our personal consciousness
should survive the change, then it would inevitably follow that the aim of life would be represented by that which is individually attainable
within the sensible limits of life.   The significance
of moral education as the preparation of characters
and powers for use in another order would cease
to exist.   If it could be shewn that the idea of a
supreme righteous Governor is against reason and
this conviction were to become current, the personal notion of pleasure would be the one standard
of appeal.   Hitherto such theories as necessity,
or absolute mortality, or atheism, have been maintained only by a few who have been at once disciplined and restrained by the influence of opposite
beliefs, but even so the issues to which they lead
have been not obscurely indicated.

The splendid visions, in which some modern
speculators have indulged, of a religion of humanity
capable of moving men to self-sacrifice and to
enthusiasm for issues indefinitely remote, seem to
be nothing but reflections of Christianity: let the
light of the Incarnation be quenched, and they
will at once vanish.   At any rate there is not the
least evidence in favour of their intrinsic and
independent efficacy over conduct.

One or two simple considerations will set this
conclusion in a clearer light. How, for example,
do we gain a moral standard of action ? If we put
out of account the belief in GOD and a future life
it does not appear what relation can be established
between different kinds of present desires and
pleasures. It may be quite true that certain general results of a character desirable for mankind
at large follow from certain lines of individual
action, but that simple fact is no adequate reason
why an individual should not, if he is able, dis-
regard these for the sake of an immediate pleasure
to himself. Why is he to sacrifice himself for
others ? Is he not, as far as he knows, the centre
and measure of things? There is at least no
sufficient evidence that the common happiness is
what any particular man is bound to prefer; and
he may fairly say that he is the sole judge of
what gives happiness to himself.

But if we introduce the idea of GOD as a
moral Governor into our view of the world, we are
constrained to believe that He will in some way
manifest Himself, and, if so, we cannot doubt that
the 'purpose' which runs through the sum of
life, though it is frequently obscured in the
individual life, is part of this manifestation. We
can then reasonably urge that the intuitions of

our own minds and the general tendencies which we observe in life are indications of His will, and thus there is at once a sufficient ground for rendering obedience to them at all cost. We cannot act as if we severally were measures of all things. The whole creation claims our regard and our service. Virtue, that is, the fulfilment of the will of GOD as it is made known to us, is a duty and not an open question.

If we pause here, the spectacle of the world is still clouded with sadness though we are no longer disturbed by uncertainty as to our duty. We go farther therefore, and take account of the idea of a future life. If this be held firmly perplexities of life at least cease to be inexplicable. It is a sufficient support in perplexity to feel that we see only a fragment of a vast scheme; for if there are signs of advance towards a harmony of creation now, there is nothing arbitrary in the supposition that hereafter the great end will be reached. We are enabled to regard the course of things, so to speak, from the side of GOD and not only from the side of man. Scope is given for the exercise of an infinite power commensurate with infinite love. Man's aspirations and failures are met by divine wisdom. Hope comes to the support of duty. There is indeed no promise of an

immediate and universal victory of good. Things
may continue in the new order to represent a
progress through conflict; but, even if we are
justified in extending to another sphere the conditions of our earthly discipline, nothing need be
lost of that which has been gained here, and the
conflict will to this extent be continued under
more favourable conditions.

In this way we can see how a belief in the
moral government of GOD and in a future life—
partial and preliminary solutions of the problems
of humanity—influence action, and give stability
and a certain grandeur to the ideas by which
modern society is ruled; but so far we obtain no
light upon our connexion one with another, or
upon the conflict between the elements of our
own nature and the disorders without us and
within us. For this we must look to revelation.
And here the light which we need flows, and, as I
believe, flows only from the fact of the Incarnation.
If then we pass from the intuitional to the
historical elements of religion, in order to realise
the practical effect of belief upon conduct, it
becomes evident that if we hold that the Son of
GOD took man's nature upon Him, we recognise a
new and ineffaceable relation between man and
man. We are assured by that fact that what

binds us together is stronger than all that tends to separate us: that there is in all men a potentiality of blessedness beyond our imagination: that the unity of the race is something more than an abstraction. Love comes to quicken hope.

And, still more than this, the same fact presents the disorders of life as intrusive and remediable, as being the violation of our nature and not belonging to its essence. The Incarnation exhibits to us the purpose of Creation consummated in a glory won through voluntary humiliation and suffering. This belief carries with it momentous consequences. It shews evil in its final character as sin, lawlessness, selfishness, so conquered for us that we can appropriate the fruits of the conquest. In the Passion and in the Resurrection we see the last issues of life, as it were, from man's side and from the side of GOD; and we welcome the assurance that human self-assertion is powerless before Divine love. Faith comes to crown life.

These simple illustrations will shew how our view of the solution of the problems of life in its broadest aspect must have a deep practical significance for each one who accepts any particular solution of them and so far as he accepts it.

But the effect of the solution does not stop with the man who has appropriated it. It extends through him to a wider circle. Personal belief alone can leaven society. Popular opinion depends for its vitality upon the intensity of individual opinion. And though an opinion which has once found acceptance commonly retains its form for a time when its real supports have been removed; yet, if it be so, the collapse when it comes, will be more startling and complete. The reflection needs to be laid to heart at the present time, because there is a growing inclination on the part of many influential teachers to represent the morality of Christianity as independent of the theology of Christianity. No judgment can be more at variance with the teaching of history. Our civilisation both in its gentleness and in its strength is due to the Christian faith and has been supported by Christian institutions. Whatever we owe to non-Christian sources comes to us through a Christian atmosphere and is steeped in Christian thought. The form must soon pass into corruption if the spirit be withdrawn. We may then be reasonably stirred to self-questioning when we observe everywhere a general vagueness in religious thought, an unconscious appropriation of results apart from their conditions. The necessity of analysing our convictions and of test-

ing the application of them is forced upon us.
Our Creed may be but a mere vesture cast over
a dead figure and not an inspiring power: it
may be only the ghost of a faith which we have
killed.

This being so it may be worth while to carry
the illustrations which I have taken one degree
farther in definition. The same law which holds
good of the effect of the ideas of GOD, and of a
future life and of the Incarnation in their most
general form, holds good also of the details of the
view under which they are realised. Let the idea
of GOD be extended so as to include not only the
notion of a righteous government but also that
of a present and personal relationship with man.
We shall see at once that the aspect of the
world will be changed. The conviction of the
possibility of obtaining help in the arduous work
of life will be added to the conviction of the
paramount claims of virtue. Prayer will become
a reality.

Substitute again the Christian doctrine of
the Resurrection of the Body for the heathen
guess of the Immortality of the Soul, and the
effect upon life will be only limited by our power
of realising the truth. The future will in a true

sense be made present. The conviction of continuity will be extended to all the elements of our being without being confined to any special organisation in which they are united. Actions and words will be guided and disciplined at every moment by a living consciousness of their inevitable endurance with us as parts of ourselves.

Or again: if we pass from the general statement of the fact of the Incarnation to the more precise apprehension of the conditions under which it is presented to us, we shall see that each typical mode of expressing the truth must carry with it corollaries of far-reaching importance. It is not an indifferent detail of scholasticism whether we place the Lord's Personality in His human or in His Divine nature. Our view of the Atonement and our conception of our own relation to the Father will depend upon it. Nothing at first sight could appear more remote from practice than the question whether the Lord's human nature is individually personal or not. Yet more careful reflection shews that our true sense of our own relation to Him as our Head depends upon the fact that He is not one man among many men, but *the One* in whom all find their fragmentary being made capable of reconciliation in a higher Personality.

It would be easy to pursue these considerations into still minuter details. Patient investigation will shew that no doctrine can be without a bearing upon action. It is of course possible to petrify a doctrine into an outward formula: to change that into a mere cloke which ought to be an informing force : but this degradation of a Creed springs from the inability or unwillingness of men to treat it as a thing of life and not from the inherent character of the Creed itself. The influence of a dogma may be good or bad—that is an important criterion of dogma with which we are not now concerned—but if the dogma be truly maintained it will have a moral value of some kind. Every religion, and every sect of every religion, has its characteristic form of life, and if the peculiarities of these forms are smoothed away by time it is only because the type of belief to which they correspond has ceased to retain its integrity and sharpness. Or to go back to the point from which we started. As long as an opinion on any of the great mysteries of self, the world and God is a reality for those who entertain it, and not a conventional phrase, it will be a moral power.

And, as we have seen, we are so made that we must inquire into these mysteries or receive

opinions on them from others. We cannot as a
matter of fact avoid speculating or acting upon
judgments as to the questions Whence? What?
Whither? We cannot, without a forcible effort,
acquiesce in the conclusion that the questions are
insoluble enigmas. If we do acquiesce in it, our
whole life will be modified by the confession of
blank negation. On the other hand, it is at our
peril that we rest in false or imperfect answers.
Error and imperfection in such a case must issue
in lives which are faulty or maimed where they
might have been nobler and more complete. The
opinions which a man holds are important positively and negatively: positively, if the opinions
find their corresponding expression in action, negatively, if they be retained as a mere fashion of
thought, and so be emptied of their natural power.
Right Doctrine is an inexhaustible spring of
strength if it be translated into deed: it is a
paralysis if it be held as an intellectual notion.
Nor can we conceive any impediment to the
fulfilment of duty more fatal than the outward
retention of a formal Creed under such conditions
that each article in it is maintained deliberately
in theory without regard to its moral realisation.

iii. It is, I repeat, a necessity of our nature
and of our circumstances that we should deal in

some way with the great mysteries of being; and
yet further it cannot but be that if we deal with
them honestly and thoroughly our theories will
influence our conduct.

It may however be said that whatever theory
we hold, observation and experience will impose
upon us the same general rules of action: that
even if we maintain speculatively the extremest
doctrine of necessity, we shall be treated by others,
and ourselves treat others, as free in the sense of
responsible: that if we regard the external world
as being nothing but the shadow of our own
minds, we shall still heed as carefully as other
men every 'law' of nature: that whether we refer
the order of the universe to a Supreme Lord or
not, we shall give ourselves loyally to the fulfilment of those offices which appear to be marked
out for us when we take a large view of the
general course of things.

I have already touched upon some of these
assertions; and I would again urge as a general
reply to this form of argument that the average
belief which modifies the application of speculative views to conduct is due to the presence or
to the traditional influence of personal conviction;
and that if there were any energetic and wide-
spread denial of our freedom or of the uniformity

of natural laws or of the Being of GOD, it is by
no means clear that our actual conduct would be
what it is.

But I do not wish to attempt now to point
out the limitations to which such statements as
I have supposed are subject. I am willing to
let them for the moment pass without challenge
as without acceptance. Yet even so, if they hold
true in the widest possible sense, the results
obtained do not cover the ground which belief
occupies. Such practical rules touch only upon
outward acts as subject to outward control.
They leave out of consideration some of the
most important elements which go to the formation of character. And our actions personally
are of importance only in relation to character.
It is indeed needless to insist at length upon
the momentous consequences of character. The
constitution of society is such that under every
form of government the moving power will be
in the hands of few. For these few the final
spring of power is conviction; and conviction is
the practical realisation of belief. In other words
the control of men—the capacity for guiding, and,
if need be, for coercing the ignorant, the weak and
the indifferent, for guiding that is at present the
mass of men,—will depend upon opinion which cor-

responds with a definite theory of things. And such opinion extends far beyond appreciable action. To take the first case supposed. A necessitarian and his adversary will do on the supposition exactly the same actions, and yet they will be wholly different men. Legislation again, to touch another point, cannot distinguish between the obedience of resignation and the obedience of enthusiasm; but it is obvious that there is an immeasurable difference between the citizen who accepts a burden from which he cannot escape and the citizen who believes that he is contributing of his own to the furtherance of a great cause.

The characters of two such men are practically incommensurable. Their power and their tendency to influence others are wholly different. In any great crisis they would be revealed, as being in fact what they are, whether the time of shewing them openly comes or not. Thus their potential difference with regard to society and to the future is enormous. Their actual difference in themselves with regard to the past is equally great. For the one repentance, remorse, thankfulness, devotion will be delusions to be extirpated, for the other they will be precious instruments of discipline and encouragement.

Again : it may be quite true that we shall
follow observed laws, as far as we have apprehended them, with a care proportioned to our
knowledge, whatever may be our theory of the
universe without us. But the effect of the world
upon our imagination, and through imagination
upon our character, will depend upon the view
which we take of its relation to ourselves and
to GOD. If we regard it as inextricably bound
up with man, as waiting, in some sense, for the
true fulfilment of his destiny, as suffering from
his failures, as contributing to the fulness of one
life, it is evident that our attitude towards it will
be different from that of students who acknowledge
no present moral relationship and no permanent
connexion between man and the rest of creation,
who regard the region of finite being open to us
as a field simply for intellectual research. To him
who believes that all creation is a living revelation
of GOD, that which phenomena serve to indicate
will be far more precious than that which we can
define in them by isolating parts of the moving
whole and treating them as fixed. Such a faith
in the divine life of things, which can become
most real, is capable of producing in him who
holds it habits of reverence and tenderness and
sympathy which profoundly affect his whole tone
of thought and temper and conduct. Whether

for good or for evil there is an almost infinite
difference of character between the pedlar for
whom the primrose 'a yellow primrose is and
nothing more' and the poet to whom

> the meanest flower that blows can give
> Thoughts that do often lie too deep for tears.

Again : nothing, I believe, can be more clear
than that the conclusion as to rules of action,
apart from all considerations of effective motive
and sanction, will be the same whether we follow
the method of a wide utilitarianism or base our
system of morality on intuitional ideas of right.
But though it may be, as I am ready to grant, of
no moment as to laying down rules of action what
abstract theory we hold as to the basis of morality ;
it is of the greatest moment as to character
whether we regard our rules as determined by
reference to ourselves and by what we can see
of their working, or by their relation to some
infinitely larger order in which we are a part :
whether, that is, we call a thing good because it is
seen to be useful within the present sphere of
our experience or because we hold that it is in
conformity with an absolute law of the working
of which we see as yet but little.

Reflections of the same kind apply to all

other articles of belief, even the most abstract. These have not only an effect upon outward action, but also upon those inward processes of thought and feeling which fashion our permanent constitution. In this respect what we think of things is at least as important as what we do. We are called upon in a word to pursue truth in opinion not less than truth in action : to discipline and elevate the imagination : to purify and ennoble the affections : to reach forward in every direction to a fuller and more perfect knowledge of the ways of GOD within us and without us. If then we turn aside from a reverent contemplation of the mysteries of life, if we refuse to throw upon them the light which we can gather, if we make no effort to realise their ennobling magnificence because we suppose, for the most part falsely, that their grandeur has no practical significance ; we leave undone that which, according to our opportunities, we are bound to do. We take to ourselves a mutilated character. We suffer one great part of ourselves to remain undisciplined, unstrengthened, unused, which (as we may reasonably believe) if not on earth yet in some larger field of being, will require for the fulfilment of its office, the results of that exercise which our present conditions are fitted to supply.

CHAPTER III.

OUR inquiries hitherto have established two important conclusions, (1) that we are placed in the midst of mysteries, and that we carry within ourselves mysteries, from which escape is impossible ; and (2) that we are so made and so placed that we are constrained to look upon them, to seek and to shape some solution of them, to live according as we interpret them. The problems of life, in a word, are inevitable; and the answers which they receive are of the most direct practical importance to those who render them.

We have now to consider the conditions under which the answer to these problems must be sought. And I do not think that I can better introduce what I have to say upon the subject in relation to present difficulties than by

W. G, L.   5

a reference to the famous passage of the *Novum Organum* in which Bacon sums up the prolific sources of 'the phantoms of the cave.'

These false and misleading spectres, which simulate the form of Truth, spring, he tells us, for the most part from certain prevailing views, from an excessive passion for synthesis or analysis, from a preference for some particular period in the history of the world, from "a telescopic or microscopic character" of mind. Now I am by no means prepared to maintain that we are not haunted still by spectres of the tribe, of the market and of the theatre: that we do not suffer from the preponderating influence of the objects of sense, from the misunderstanding of current terms, from the attractiveness of brilliant theories; but the spectres of the cave seem to crowd about us just now in greater numbers than all these and to disturb our judgment more deeply, partly by their fictitious terrors and partly by their unsubstantial beauty. Or to drop the image and speak plainly, there seems to be a growing danger lest all facts should be forced into one category, lest one method of investigation should be armed with an absolute despotism, lest one verifying test should be transformed into a universal necessity.

It is then of primary importance to guard ourselves against this danger when we enter upon the study of Religion or Theology. And that we may learn to do so the more completely we must still keep our attention fixed upon the broadest aspects of things. By the help of this discipline we shall be enabled at once to see that we are constrained in our speculations to distinguish several distinct groups of phenomena which rest on separate bases, which lead to results differing essentially in kind, which must be verified by characteristic proofs: to see that there are various classes of Truths which are marked not by different *degrees* of certainty, but by different *kinds* of certainty: that the word 'science' has a manifold application: that Theology is most really a positive science based upon its own special facts, and pursued according to its own proper method. The reflections which I desire to suggest will group themselves, as before, round the three final elements of being—self, the world, and GOD; and it will be my general object to shew that the type of science which belongs to each of these ultimate divisions of the objects of thought is absolutely distinct; and that each more complex science presupposes and rests upon that which is simpler and more general.

i. In the first place then a man may regard
himself alone, and isolate the laws of limitation
under which his impressions are received from
the objects which stimulate his senses.   The ideas
of time and space, of succession and extension,
when once apprehended in their most simple and
absolute form become the sufficient foundation
for wide and complicated conclusions.   When the
ideas have once been called into play, there is no
longer any need that the inquirer should turn a
single thought to phenomena.   An experiment
may illustrate one of his results, but it is impossible to conceive any experiment which could
either confirm his legitimate deductions or shake
them.   The utmost developments of the relations
of number and figure are absolute for man.   The
facts with which he deals in them are not only
assumed to be constant : for him they *are* constant.
Nothing, as long as he is what he is, can interfere
with the certainty of his deductions.   But we
must observe that we are not justified in extending
the limitations of our perceptions to any other
order of beings.   Obviously we cannot extend them
to an Infinite Being.   They may be shadows or
fragments of something larger, grander, immeasur-
ably more comprehensive, into which they are
capable of being taken up and resolved.   But
however this may be, we cannot give definiteness

to such thoughts; and we come back to the marks
of our primary group of sciences. The sphere is
man himself. The subject is the characteristic
limitations of his perceptions. The method is
deductive. The verification of the results lies in
the possibility of their resolution into elements
of which the opposite is unthinkable.

ii. But man cannot rest here. He is constrained to look continuously without. He regards
self, and he regards the world. And however
much he may be tempted to mould the phenomena
of the world into some preconceived shape, he is
soon compelled to abandon the attempt. Prior to
observation he is utterly unable to predict the
laws which represent the action of the various
forces about him. To the last he has no complete
assurance that he has detected all the forces
which are at work and ready to reveal themselves.
But by the accumulation of experience he can do
much in grouping vast series of phenomena
under adequate formulas; and just as he isolates
the abstract conditions of observation (conditions
of time and space) from the concrete facts through
which they are made known to men, he can isolate
also in imagination the operation of each force;
and when he has done so, but not till then, the
method of deduction can be applied to data which

are treated separately as absolute. The assumed
conditions are, of course, in this case imaginary;
but where the actual phenomena are resolvable
into the resultants of few elements the recurrence
of the phenomena can be predicted with an assurance proportioned to their simplicity. But the
certainty obtainable in this region is separated
by an impassable chasm from the certainty which
belongs to the former group of facts.

It reposes on a twofold assumption, which
from the nature of the case can never cease to be
an assumption. It is assumed that the observed
law is constant, and it is assumed that no force
hitherto unperceived will hereafter interfere with
the observed manifestation of the law. Now even
as things are, late physical researches as we have
already seen suggest grounds for believing that
the present state of the world could not have come
about from the uniform action of the forces which
we can now observe ; and the fact that energy is
being constantly dissipated, that is, I imagine,
stored up though not used, seems to indicate that
provision is being made for some hitherto unknown
revelation of being. Perhaps indeed, if I may
venture on a conjecture, the phenomena of physics
may be conceived of best as falling under some
vast progressive periodic cycles, an ascending

spiral as it were, though for the infinitesimal fragments of their course during which we can observe them, no appreciable error is made by assuming the constancy of the laws which express their general form.

However I have no right to enter further on this field, and all that I desire to indicate is that we have within it a new kind of phenomena, subject to new conditions only partially discoverable in their relations to ourselves, a new method of inquiry, a new test of verification. The sphere is external nature: the method is inductive: the verification is experiment and prediction: while at the same time the former sphere, the former method, the former test underlie these, and is unmodifiable by them. Physical Truth, in a word, is not homogeneous with mathematical Truth, but all physical results involve a mathematical foundation. They rest, that is, in their expression upon the limitations of succession.

But we must go further. Hitherto we have considered only the manifestation of inorganic being. All investigation tends to confirm the instinct which separates physical force from life. *Omne vivum ex vivo* is a principle which brings us face to face with a new series of phenomena. And even if future researches should shew that there is, or make it probable that there has been, an evolution of life from matter, the region of life will still remain clearly distinct. We have here to deal with the fullest development of phenomena and not with their inchoate stage. In the case of living bodies then all the observed laws of inorganic being hold good so far as these bodies can be considered simply as inorganic, but no further. All the laws which limit our observation hold good in the deductions which can be drawn from them. But life itself is an element wholly different in order from those with which we have dealt hitherto. The variety, the complexity, the cumulative transmission of its manifestations, render experiment and prediction for the most part nugatory. This is true both of the single life and of the sum of being. We cannot here, except in the broadest generalizations, assume permanence in the conditions of the problem : we cannot assume permanence in the mysterious energy of life itself: we cannot affect to leave out of consideration the interference of individual influences, which, from whatever source they spring, are at least incalculable. We find our-selves in the presence of a movement due to an immeasurable combination of concurrent or con-flicting powers. It is a grand truth that ' the

dead rule the living,' but they *rule* them and
they do no more. No despot however absolute
could destroy the personality of his subjects.

The Truth of life then, Historical Truth, must
be generically different in kind from Mathematical
or Physical Truth. Historical Truth is concerned primarily with the reality of specific facts.
Physical Truth is concerned primarily with the
coordination of groups of facts. The basis of the
one is testimony which is unique, the basis of the
other is experiment which can be repeated. The
particular incident is in the first case a fragment
of a continuous growth, in the second it is an
example of that which is for us an unchanging
law. No doubt our conviction of Physical Truth
and of Historical Truth agrees in this that in both
cases the conviction admits of degrees of certainty,
but the degrees depend upon wholly different
conditions. The adequacy of the testimony is
the measure of historical certainty : the adequacy
of the experiments is the measure of physical
certainty.

Here then we have a new science. The sphere
is human life, the method is the investigation of
the records of the past and present: the verification rests on testimony taken in connexion with

the analogy of experience. I am not concerned
to inquire why we are so constituted as to believe
testimony any more than why we are so constituted
as to accept a universal statement based upon a
limited induction. What seems to be of chief
importance is, that being what we are, we do and
must accept as true facts which we cannot bring to
the test of experiment, facts which by their very
nature are incapable of repetition. It is simply
impossible to apply to history the method or the
test of physics: but certainty is equally attainable
in both cases for the uses of human life, though it
represents the result of different processes.

iii. I have touched upon what appear to
be the characteristics of the different kinds of
certainty corresponding respectively with the
conclusions which flow from the limitations of our
own nature, from our direct observation, according
to these limitations of the inorganic world, and
from the indirect record of the past experience of
life. But there is yet another sphere of knowledge. The existence of the personal 'I' and of
the external world are two self-luminous truths.
And there is also a third, which rests, as we have
seen, on the same foundation of consciousness,
that is, the Being of GOD. In other words man
stands in a present and abiding relationship with

an unseen and eternal as well as with a seen and
temporal order. His individual life is directly
connected with a vaster life which is its source,
and the world on which he looks is part of a
universe of being which is made known through it
only partially, if really. Here then there is room
for another type of Truth, for another method of
inquiry, for another kind of certainty. We are
brought to the threshold of a new science, the
positive science of Theology, which like the
other sciences must have its own appropriate
facts. How then can we obtain these facts ? How
can we be assured that they are facts ? How can
we use them as the basis of further deductions
and generalisations ?

Before I attempt to answer these questions
I must mark three laws which we have observed in our consideration of the mathematical,
physical, and vital sciences. The first is, that the
fundamental facts of each science and of each
type of science are in themselves respectively
independent of every other science and of every
other type of science. We cannot, for instance,
predict by the help of any deductions from the
conceptions of time and space what will be the
character of the solar system. The law of gravitation again cannot form the sufficient basis of

the law of chemical combination or of laws of
action. There may be an undiscovered unity, as
there is certainly a marvellous harmony, between
the different laws when they are approximately
understood, but it is impossible to pass directly
from one science to another. The attempt to do
so would be an attempt on a greater or less scale
to construct a world *à priori*.

The second law is, that in any complex phenomenon we can isolate by abstraction those
elements which belong to the domain of a particular science, and then the law and method of the
particular science will *so far* find a right and
complete application to the phenomenon in question. For example, if the hand describes a curve
under definite conditions, we may consider the
figure only : or the action of gravity upon the
limb while describing it, both *in vacuo* and in a
resisting medium of an assumed or of a determined character : or the internal changes in the
living frame attendant upon the action : or the
record of the movement given by a spectator.
The problems which are thus raised are perfectly
distinct and must be treated independently if we
are to obtain a true conception of the whole
action. Physiology is unable to fix the properties

of the curve, and conversely geometry throws no light on the processes of life.

The third law is, that the method which is followed in the pursuit of Truth is essentially different in the groups of sciences which belong to self and to the world. The method which deals with the problems involved in the universal, limitations of human observation is intuitive as to the fundamental facts and deductive in the application of them : the method which deals with the problems of the world whether physical or vital is inductive, and depends for its fundamental facts upon observation and testimony, confirmed in the one case by direct experiment and prediction, and in the other, in the largest sense, by general experience. The facts can be used as the certain basis of a deductive process only so far as it is assumed in a particular case that the phenomena with which they correspond are perfectly known and constant.

If now we apply these laws to the science of Theology we shall have advanced some way towards the answer to the questions which have been proposed. We shall expect that the facts which belong to Theology as a special science will be derived from some other source than the analysis of the conditions of thought or the observation of the uniformities of the world: that there will be some ultimate faculty in man capable of deciding with certainty upon the questions with which it deals: that different elements in these complex facts through which a revelation is given may be isolated and dealt with separately, but no partial investigation of the facts, so far as they fall within the domain of the inferior sciences can determine their theological value.

i. Such conclusions are justified by reflection and experience. For while we feel no less surely that GOD is than that we are and that the world is, and are conscious of an affinity to Him, we cannot come to a knowledge of Him from the interrogation of ourselves or of nature. We cannot deduce from an examination of our own constitution what He must be. This would be impossible in any case for an imperfect and finite creature; and if the creature be also fallen and sinful the impossibility is intensified. We must then look without ourselves for the knowledge of GOD. But here again we cannot command at our pleasure adequate sources of information. Experiment is capable only of rare application to the complicated phenomena of life and it can have no place in regard to the will of an Infinite Being. If then we are to know GOD, He must

in His own way make Himself known to us, and
we on our part must be able to recognise and to
give a personal welcome to the revelation.

It does not appear to be necessary to discuss
the question whether GOD can reveal Himself
to man, or rather whether man *continuing to be
what he is* can receive a revelation of GOD.
The possibility of a revelation is included in the
idea which we have of GOD; and finds a characteristic expression in the belief that man was
made "in the image of GOD." This original idea
belongs, as we have assumed, to the fulness of the
individual life; and it is realised more and more
fully through life. It does not obtain its mature
form at once either for the individual or for the
race. It follows therefore that if a revelation be
given to man it must also come to him through
life. It will be addressed, that is, to the whole
man and not to a part of man, as (for example) to
the intellect or to the affections. It will, in other
words, be presented in facts and not in words
only. Man will learn to know more and more
of GOD—and this is the teaching of history and
experience—not by purely intellectual processes,
but by intercourse with Him, by listening to His
voice and interpreting the signs which He gives
of His presence and His will.

These facts of revelation then, these 'signs' (σημεῖα) in the language of the New Testament, are the fundamental facts of Theology. Either in themselves or from the circumstances of their occurrence they are such as to suggest the immediate presence or action of GOD, of a personal power producing results not explicable by what we observe in the ordinary course of nature. They are not properly proofs of a teaching from which they are dissociated, but the teaching itself in a limited form which appeals to men through human experience. They have a spiritual power, and, so far, they are 'spiritually discerned' while the intellect prepares the way for this discernment. They indicate in all cases something of the connexion between the seen and the unseen. Theology, even in its simplest form, claims to set forth this connexion; and Christian Theology, to take the completest example, of which every other Theology is in some measure a preparation or a reflex, offers to us this connexion definitely established for ever in a historical manifestation of GOD—in the Incarnation and Passion and Resurrection of the Lord—which as it extends to the whole of life opens also an inexhaustible fountain of wisdom as our knowledge of life becomes deeper and wider.

Thus the historical facts through which the Christian Revelation is given, are the spiritual facts of Christian Theology, which are added to what we know or can know of GOD from other sources. The events which are proclaimed as human contain also an emphatic declaration of something transcendental, of an atonement, a restored union of man and of humanity and of the world with GOD in Christ.

On one side these signs—the special manifestations of the action of GOD and consequently of His character and purposes—are facts. So far they fall within the domain of history, and are subject to the ordinary laws of historical investigation. But they are more than facts which belong to the visible order. As facts which belong to the visible order they can be investigated by the ordinary methods of criticism, but something will still remain to be apprehended by a spiritual faculty. They have a historic side inasmuch as they are events in human life, but no simply historic process can lay open their inner significance. They are capable again of a logical interpretation, but no system of deductive exposition can supersede the vital apprehension of the facts themselves. The facts which are the foundation of Theology are suggested by but are not identical with the external phenomena through which we are made acquainted with them. They are, as is obvious in the case of the Resurrection, an interpretation of the phenomena. The outward facts become facts in this higher sense, truths without ceasing to be facts.

ii. How then can we be assured that these facts are facts not only in their historical but also in their spiritual aspect? The law of testimony will carry us to a conclusion as to the outward phenomenon. How can we be sure of its divine import? I do not hesitate to reply that we are by nature made capable of judging on this point also.

Nor is the assumption of the existence of such a power of recognition, of apprehension, of interpretation of the divine, at variance with what we have noticed hitherto. So far from this being so, the assumption corresponds with what we have actually seen in the case of induction and testimony, which serve as the foundations of physical and historical certainty. It is in no way more surprising that I should say when a moral principle is presented to me, I acknowledge this as of absolute obligation, or when a unique occurrence is related to me, I acknowledge this as a divine message, than that I should say such an event has happened so many times, and therefore it will happen again, or so and so told me and therefore I believe him. The conclusion in each case seems to answer to our ultimate constitution. And though the term Faith is properly applied to the power by which we gain data as to the unseen and eternal order, there is something directly corresponding to Faith in the power by which we accept general conclusions as to what we call 'laws' of Nature and special conviction as to events of history which are equally removed from the test of sense (comp. p. 28).

The proof of Revelation is then primarily personal. It springs from a realised fellowship with the unseen which we are enabled to gain. The two complementary statements *credo ut intelligam* (*fides præcedit intellectum*) and *intelligo ut credam* are both true at different points in the divine life. The one applies to the groundwork; the other to the superstructure: the one describes the apprehension of the fundamental facts; the other describes the expression of doctrines. Faith obtains the new data for reasoning, but when the data are firmly held, then the old methods become applicable. Historical facts convey new lessons when regarded in the light of the revealed

relation of GOD to the world; and, within certain
limits, we can express conclusions in human language which present the truth adequately for us.
The data do not modify these methods, but increase the materials to which they are applicable.

Revelation, in a word, which gives us the
characteristic data of Theology in a history,
inasmuch as it comes from without us, and our
being is one, presupposes and rests upon the
deductive laws which express the limitation
of our thoughts, and the inductive laws which
express our apprehension of the phenomena of
life and nature, and the laws of historical criticism by which we investigate the records of the
past, though it has also its own peculiar method
of proof. Nor is the additional process, if we may
so call it, by which we gain assurance in this
region of knowledge through faith more different
from the inductive process by which we gain
moral certainty in regard to the outward world of
sense, or the process of historical criticism by
which we gain moral certainty as to fresh events,
than the latter processes themselves are different
from the deductive process which establishes de-
monstratively the consequences of the constitution
of our own minds. The four or (three) processes
correspond to four (or three) different orders of

existences; and that which extends farthest includes the results of those which deal with more
limited ranges of thought.

And though the proof of revelation is finally
personal, the correspondence of the character of
the revelation with the general instincts and
tendencies of humanity, with what the experience
of life on a large scale teaches us as to the
constitution of the individual and of the race,
gives a certain universality to the proof.   At the
same time the 'signs' of revelation do not stand
as isolated events in the history of the world.
They also are above all things interpretative
events.   They illustrate what was before dark,
and combine what was before scattered.   They
let in light to our order in such a way as to
convey the conviction that there is an order of
perfect light which is not inaccessible by us.

These considerations meet the difficulty which
comes from the variety of the interpretations of
the subject-matter of revelation.   The conviction
which is primarily personal is brought to a social
trial.   We cannot reduce the propositions in which
it is expressed to elements of which the opposite
is unthinkable.   We cannot bring them to a
definite experiment.   We must try them finally

by the test of life. And that may be justly
accepted as the highest truth for man, which
is shewn to be capable of calling out, disciplining,
sustaining, animating with the noblest activity all
the powers of man in regard to self, the world and
GOD, under the greatest variety of circumstances.
If anything human lies without the scope of a
revelation to man, that revelation cannot be final.

iii. We have seen that while the characteristic
element in the facts which form the basis of
Theology does not fall within the range of historical investigation, the same law holds good in
the case of Theology which we have observed
before. The higher science includes all that
precede, as being at once subordinate and preparatory to it. The science for example which
deals with the action of bodies one upon another
assumed to be unchanged in themselves, is included in that which deals with the action of body
upon body when both are supposed to be under-
going change. The science of life, to rise upwards,
which takes account of phenomena peculiar to
itself, treats of them in accordance with all the
laws observed in inorganic bodies. When again
we pass to that more complex form of human
existence which for the want of a proper word
we call the life of nations, and at last the life

of humanity, this, which proceeds according to its own laws, is subject no less in due measure to all the laws which regulate individual existence. So too it is with the science of morality which deals with the highest problems of social and personal life as they are conditioned by the circumstances of our present existence. So too it is at last with Theology. This carries us indeed into a higher order. It has facts and laws of its own; but these are underlaid by all the other laws which determine our powers of observation and our relation to one another and to the order in which we live.

In this universal principle we have the answer to our third question. Theology has Truths of which no other science can judge: but though the fulness of these truths belongs exclusively to Theology, still Theology does not deal with them as supramundane from their divine side, but so far as they are appreciable under the conditions of our present existence, so far as they are operative in the many phases of our actual experience. They are in all respects relative to the order which is opened to our inquiry and observation, and connect this with an order into which we cannot ourselves penetrate. They treat of the infinite reconciled to the finite and

not of the infinite in the abstract, of GOD united
with man, and not of GOD in Himself. It is
therefore evident that the apprehension of the
Christian revelation, as a revelation, presupposes
an evergrowing acquaintance with that form of
being in and through which it is given. The facts
of revelation do not in themselves and cannot constitute a theory of the external world, so far as
it is offered to us for investigation by our present
powers, but they connect such a theory, which is
the final goal of all intellectual effort, with that
which is unseen and eternal. Step by step we
come to know better the constitution of man, the
laws of society, the interdependence of the parts of
the material universe; and exactly as we advance
in this knowledge, we can understand with surer
confidence and deeper insight the import of the
revelation made known to us in the Life of Christ,
and in the mission of the Holy Spirit, whereby
man and society and the universe are placed in a
living union with GOD. And thus all the knowledge which we can gain of the finite, all the
knowledge which we can gain of man, extends
and illuminates our knowledge of GOD, Who has
been made known to us through the finite and
in the Person of Him Who was perfect Man.
Nothing therefore which enlarges our acquaintance with creation in its widest sense can be

indifferent to the Theologian : to him every access
of truth is, in a secondary sense, a revelation ; or to
the Christian, more exactly, a comment on the one
absolute revelation. So it is that Theology becomes
the soul of Religion. Theology is a science and
Religion is the fulness of life. Theology is the
crown of all the sciences, and Religion is the
synthesis of all.

But, as I have already said, the method of
each subsidiary science must be used only so far
as it is applicable. Physics will lead us to a
certain point : physiology will carry us yet further :
history will carry us still onwards : revelation will
add that element of infinity to knowledge which
gives characteristic permanence to every work and
thought. Each science is supreme within its own
domain. But no science can arrogate to itself the
exclusive possession of certainty or Truth. Nor
does it appear that there is any virtue in the
power of vivid illustration which belongs to
Physics, for example, such as to distinguish
physical conclusions as certain, when compared
with the conclusions of ethics or theology. It
is rather narrowness than precision of thought
which confines the word knowledge to the facts
which we reach in a particular way; and the
student seems to wilfully abridge his heritage who

pronounces all that 'unknowable' which is not
accessible by one kind of machinery.

Each science, I repeat, is supreme within its
own domain; but it has no sovereign authority
beyond it. The certainty which man can obtain
and by which he lives is manifold in kind and
corresponds with each separate region of phenomena. There is no one method of obtaining
Truth: there is no one universal test of Truth.
No process can lead to a complete result in a
different order from that to which it properly
belongs. No conclusion from the science of
matter or of life can (as far as I can see) establish
any conclusion as to a point in morals or theology
and conversely. A physical law will help us to
present to our minds more distinctly a spiritual
fact: a spiritual fact will illuminate the relations
of a physical law to the moral order of the
universe; but the two are absolutely distinct
in their nature and in their sphere.

At the same time from the inherent constitution of the hierarchy of Truths there is
always a serious danger lest a method which
happens to be eminently clear and dominant
should come to be regarded as absolute and
universal. The danger is the greater if the

method is openly successful in dealing with
the phenomena to which it is peculiarly appropriate. In the early and middle ages the popular
method of Theology usurped authority over
Physics; and now the established methods of
Physics or of Biology usurp authority over Theology. As we look back we can see plainly the
fatal errors of the past: it is more difficult to see
the equally fatal errors which are active about us
now.

And yet in one important respect the present
confusion of methods is more perilous than that
old confusion which we can at length unhesitat-
ingly condemn. There is more likelihood that
a method which is truly applicable in part
should be regarded as decisively adequate than
that a method wholly inapplicable should continue
to be used. And each successive zone of phenomena (so to speak) of greater complexity admits
of being treated up to a certain point by the
method appropriate to the zone immediately
below, because it includes those phenomena as
the foundation upon which new data are super-
added. In such a case therefore the imperfect
treatment is, as far as it goes, sound and
attractive, but it is essentially incomplete. The
results are defective exactly in that which is

characteristic of the true results, while they are otherwise true in themselves. But on the other hand if the methods appropriate to a higher zone are applied to a lower, then the results are wholly fictitious.

Both these faulty methods of procedure have, as has been already noticed, been actually carried into effect. The method of Theology has been applied to Physics, and the issue was mere dreams; and now the method of Physics is applied to Theology, and the result must be of necessity the denial of all that is peculiar to Theology.

True Theologians therefore will strive to guard themselves alike against the temptation to refuse to other sciences the fullest scope as far as they reach, and against the temptation to acknowledge that they are finally authoritative over that which does not come within their range. They will not withdraw one document which helps to define their faith from the operation of any established law of criticism, but they will refuse to admit that any historical inquiry can decide that there is no revelation. They will refuse to accept as an axiom (or a postulate) that every record which attests a revelation must be false.

CHAPTER IV.

THE WORK OF THE PRE-CHRISTIAN NATIONS TO-WARDS THE SOLUTION OF THE PROBLEMS OF LIFE.

WE have already seen in a rapid survey what are the typical mysteries which underlie human life, what are the forces which constrain us to consider them, what are the conditions under which we must seek for their solution. Christianity—the Gospel of the Resurrection—is as I have already said the complete answer to all our questionings, so far as we can receive an answer at present, an answer which we are slowly spelling out through the growing experience of the life of the Church. But before this complete answer was given other answers were made, partial and tentative, which offer for our study the most solemn aspect of ancient history. Some of these answers I propose now to examine summarily. If we can in any way apprehend them clearly, we shall understand better than by any other method both the wants of man, and the resources which he has himself for supplying them, and the extent to which his natural endowments are able to satisfy his wants.

But before we endeavour to characterise the chief solutions which have been proposed for the riddle of life apart from Christianity, it is necessary to define again the character of the solution which we require, and to determine the general principles on which we may treat the religions of the world as ancillary to and illustrative of the gospel.

We require then briefly a religious solution: a solution which shall deal with the great questions of our being and our destiny in relation to thought and action and feeling. The Truth at which we aim must take account of the conditions of existence and define the way of conduct. It is not for speculation only: so far Truth is the subject of philosophy. It is not for discipline only: so far it is the subject of ethics. It is not for embodiment only: so far it is the subject of ·art. Religion in its completeness is the harmony of the three, philosophy, ethics, and art, blended into one by a spiritual power, by a consecration at once personal and absolute. The direction of

philosophy, to express the thought somewhat
differently is theoretic and its end is the True,
as the word is applied to knowledge: the direction
of Ethics is practical, and its end is the Good: the
direction of Art is representative, and its end is
the Beautiful. Religion includes these three ends
but adds to them that in which they find their
consecration, the Holy. The Holy brings an
infinite sanction and meaning to that which is
otherwise finite and relative. It expresses not
only a complete inward peace but also an essential fellowship with GOD.

The perfect religion, the perfect solution of
the mysteries of life, will offer these elements and
aims in absolute adjustment and efficacy; and each
element and aim will exist, at least in a rudi-
mentary form, in every religion. But from our
inherent incompleteness and faultiness now one
element and now another will be unduly promi-
nent. It may be thought or will or feeling which
is in excess, and then there will follow the dangers
of dogmatism or moralism or mysticism. Every
religion and every age offers illustrations of such
one-sided developments; and it is easy to see
through these very exaggerations that if religion
is to correspond with the fulness of life the three
constituents are essential to its complete activity;

and that each one severally needs the other two
for its own proper realisation.

Such considerations serve also to indicate a
comprehensive definition of religion.   It has
been defined as the consciousness of dependence :
as right action; and as knowledge.   In these
several conceptions there is some confusion from
the fundamental differences in the point of sight
from which religion may be regarded.   Religion
may be regarded as a tendency, a potential
energy or faculty in man, or as a system, a
view, of life corresponding to some stage of the
development of this tendency, or as the external
expression which it finds in personal conduct.
Thus all the definitions given above contain a
fragment of truth though they deal severally with
one side of the truth only.   All point to a harmony
of being as the final aim towards which man
reaches out as born for religion, and which religions seek to represent in some partial and yet
intelligible form.   Even the rudest demon-worship
contains the germ of this feeling by which the
worshipper seeks to be at one with some power
which is adverse to him.   It is a witness to something in man by which he is naturally constituted
to feel after a harmonious fellowship with all that
of which he is conscious, with the unseen, and

with the infinite, no less than with the seen and the material.

From one side then religion may be defined to be the active expression of that element in man, or rather perhaps of his whole being more or less concordantly united, by which he strives to realise a harmony in all things: and, from the other side, a religion is that view of all things which corresponds under particular circumstances with his nature as constituted to seek after this harmony.

Starting then from the idea of a perfect harmony as the final aim of religion, we see that its immediate purpose is to bind together that which is scattered, as things are, or discordant, and to reunite that which has been disarranged or severed. This being so it is evident that in order to reach to the full breadth of the conception of religion we must go beyond man himself. Not only is there a division and discord in self: there is also a division and discord between self and the world, and between self and GOD. Religion claims to deal with these external discords no less than with the discord within us. Religion must be capable of bringing reconciliation and order to those elements and relations of our being which give rise to the widest and most enduring conflicts. It must take account of the continuity of life by

which we are united with the past and with the
future. It must take account of the solidarity of
life by which at any one time we are united in
one real whole. It must take account of the
totality of life by which all the parts of creation
are united in a mutual, though dimly seen, interdependence. And thus we come at last to a
general notion of its office to reconcile, to coordinate, to discipline, to hallow: to reconcile
man and GOD, to coordinate man and the world,
to discipline the individual, to hallow all life by
the recognition of a divine presence and a divine
will.

This then is our first point: we require for the
satisfaction of wants which belong to our constitution a religious solution of the mysteries by which
we are surrounded: a solution which shall bring into
a harmonious relation the past, the present, and the
future, the seen and the unseen, the conflicting
elements of our personal nature. The facts of
personal and social life lead us to expect that the
end which we are made to seek will not be reached
without long and painful efforts, without failures,
partial attainments, relapses. They encourage us
to believe that nothing will be lost in which the
spirit of man has answered however imperfectly
to the Spirit of GOD. They move us to read as

we can the lessons of human experience in the slow unfolding of religious ideas, for the widening and strengthening of our divine convictions.

We turn therefore to the long records of the past to learn how men have solved or rather have tried to solve the problems which, as we have seen, must meet them more or less distinctly in the course of life. The past is in this respect the portraiture of humanity. It shews what man is and what he strives to gain. We could not have determined *a priori* what form these final questions of being would take, and still less what answers would be rendered to them. Each man is only able to realise a small fragment of the wants, the feelings, the aspirations of the race. But in the accumulated experience of ages we see legibly written the fuller tendencies, the more varied strivings, the manifold failures and victories of our common nature. The religious character of man no less than his social or his intellectual character is to be sought, not in speculation first, but in the actual observation of the facts of his continuous development.

This consideration alone must be sufficient to impress upon the student of Christian Theology the necessity of striving, as opportunity may be given, to understand the essential ideas of faiths, however strange or even repulsive, in which his fellow-men have lived and died. These faiths all shew something of what man is, and of what man has made of man, though GOD be not far from each one. The religious history of the world is the very soul of history; and it speaks to the soul. It speaks perhaps with eloquent pathos through some isolated monument which is the sole record of a race that has passed away, as, for example, through those figures from Easter Island in front of which we pass to the treasures of our British Museum. That epitome of a 'Natural Theology' wrought in stone is a fitting preface to the records of human achievement throughout the ages.

Such a search for the religious characteristics of man in the past history of religion is in many respects parallel to the search for the intellectual characteristics of man in the history of the many languages through which the divided nations have expressed their thoughts. A religion and a language even in their simplest forms are witnesses to necessities of man's constitution, and in some sense they are also prophecies of the fuller satisfaction which the wants out of which they spring will obtain in due time. No one language exhausts man's capacity for defining, combining, subordinating objects of thought, but all languages together give a lively and rich picture of his certain and yet gradual advance in innumerable different paths towards the fulness of intellectual development. So too it is with the many faiths and observances which men have spontaneously adopted. These in due measure reveal something of his religious powers and needs.

Each race bears actual historical witness to the reality of some particular phase of religious opinion: of noble endeavour as it may be, or of disastrous delusion, or of sad defeat, or of advancing conquest. And if this be so we shall in a certain degree approximate towards a true conception of the religion which corresponds with man's nature by a review of the religious strivings of the many nations. In their experience lies a witness which cannot be gainsaid.

This relation between the history of languages and the history of religion is more than a simple parallel. Religion and language have points of close connexion. This connexion has sometimes been rated too highly and sometimes misinterpreted but it cannot be overlooked with impunity. Natural groups of religions and natural groups of languages are generally coincident. Nor is it strange that it should be so. The same intellectual peculiarities which fix the formation of a language, will fix also the formation of the re-

ligious belief, so far as it is an object of thought.
The prevalent mode of viewing the world will
make itself felt both in language and in religion.
It is, for example, to take the simplest of all
instances, a point of vast moment in the construc-
tion of a popular religious faith whether in the
language of the people persons and things are
alike distinguished by sex-termination, or are
separated from the first into distinct classes. In
the one case there is the possibility of the personification of natural powers from which flow
almost necessarily the rich imaginations of mythology. In the other case the possibility is
excluded.

The effect of the absence or presence of this
capacity and tendency to personify external objects
is seen both in the general form of religious belief,
and specially in the names given to the unseen
powers. Two great types of the worship of the
African races are determined by this difference.
The worship of the Kafirs, Negroes and Poly-
nesians, who have no distinction of sex in nouns, is
a worship of ancestors, the personal beings whom
they can realise through memory; the worship of
the Hottentots and North African races is based
on the personification of the heavenly bodies sug-

gested by their sex-denoting languages[1]. So again in Chinese there are no genders and there is no indigenous mythology.

Again, when men give names to the unseen forms by which they believe that they are surrounded they may seek them either from what they observe in human action or from the phenomena of the outer world. The Shemitic and Aryan religions are distinguished by this fundamental difference of view. The Divine names which are proper to the Shemitic languages are predicative and moral, drawn from the relations of human society: the names which are proper to the Aryan languages are physical and concrete[2]. But here it is evident that the language does not mould the fashion of the thought but simply reveals it. The idea of the Divine power is realised in the one case under the image of a moral relation and in the other under a physical image. We can say no more than that both modes of representing the

[1] Dr Bleek, *Comparative Grammar of the South African Languages*, Preface, quoted by Max Müller, *Introduction to the Science of Religion*, pp. 40 f.; and compare for the whole subject Max Müller's Essay in his ' *Chips*,' ii. pp. 1—146.

[2] The Chinese represent both conceptions. Of the two names which they apply to the highest spiritual powers the one expresses the thought of physical vastness with an unalterable simplicity and (it may be said) incompleteness (*Tien*), and the other that of supreme sovereignty (*Ti, Shang Ti.*)

ultimate fact are essentially human, and necessary
for its complete expression. An absolute religion
will in some way recognise both.

If we go a step further in the development of
language, and proceed from the mere giving of
names to the formation of words we shall find that
the structural differences of languages—which
answer to specialities of national character—exert
a direct influence upon the growth of religious
beliefs. Our example shall be taken again from
a comparison of the Shemitic and Aryan languages.

In the Shemitic languages the root, the fundamental element of the word, stands out with
ineffaceable distinctness: in the Aryan languages
the root is often covered up in formative elements.
This great law extends even to a secondary stage.
In Hebrew, for example, with one or two doubtful exceptions, there are absolutely no compound
words: in· Greek and German, to take the most
familiar examples, the power and richness of the
language depends in a great measure upon the
limitless variety of compounds. In the former
case therefore the original meaning of the root so
to speak shines through the dress in which it is
clothed, and the resultant word always points back
to its source. In the latter case, the derivatives
often become names which have lost their signi-

ficance, and which call up none of their first
associations. In the Shemitic dialects the terms
for the *heaven* or the *dawn* could not put off their
direct physical meaning. The personal interpretation of the phenomena of nature was thus
impossible. With the Aryan languages it was
otherwise. The meaning of Eos or Hecate, of
Jupiter or Mars was forgotten; and the manifestations of one unknown Power were made separate
personalities. The general conclusion from these
facts has been well summed up in a single
sentence: "The language of the Shemitic races
was theological: the language of the Aryan races
was mythological" (Max Müller).

This difference carried with it far-reaching
consequences. In the one case there was, if not
the tendency, at least the power to concentrate
the different ideas of majesty and lordship on
One Sovereign: in the other case there was the
tendency to define and isolate the separate representations of forces regarded in their outward
manifestations.

But while we recognise the part which language has played and still plays in giving form
to popular religious notions, we must be careful
not to exaggerate this influence. The language
does not itself create or finally explain the religion.

It simply illustrates the impulses and tendencies which found expression in the religion under the intellectual form; but the impulses and tendencies themselves underlie religion and language alike. We have not reached the end when we can see that particular languages offered facilities for the formation and propagation of special religious ideas. The original question still remains: How came the languages to have these peculiar developments? And the answer remains hidden in the ultimate mystery of life. Language reveals the deepest springs of thought, and of religious thought as of all other thought, but it does not create them. Each particular language reveals, or has the tendency to reveal, just so much of the Truth as the race is endowed with as a constituent of humanity. Man is born to worship just as he is born to speak: he is born religious just as he is born social. In the ordering of outward life he finds expression for the one part of his nature: in the embodiment of faith he finds expression for the other. The consciousness of the three fundamental existences—self, the world, GOD—carries with it necessarily the desire to reconcile them. That this is so is an ultimate fact of experience.

To go back then to the point from which we digressed, we are justified in looking to history

for a manifestation of man's nature, originally
religious, shewn in many fragments and under
many disguises. A belief in GOD constrains us
to hold that the office of working out different
parts of the total inheritance of mankind was
committed in the order of Providence to different
races. And in every part, in every fragmentary
realisation of man's endowments and powers, religion has a share. Religion is necessary for the
full expression of human life. In the course of
time, under isolating influences, systems of philosophy or morals or art may usurp the place of
religion, but even so they render a silent homage
to its sovereignty. They shew something of the
depths of the soul over which religion broods;
and stir thoughts, efforts, feelings, which they
cannot satisfy. They treat, if only partially, of
mysteries of GOD, the world, and self, which lie in
the innermost consciousness of men. Their division is a witness to the developed vastness of the
thoughts which they cannot keep together. But
at first men strive after a religious interpretation
of phenomena dimly seen. Little by little the religious idea takes shape, often falsely and always
imperfectly. The embodiment grows and decays
with the society to which it corresponds; but
each stage of growth and decay—of growth, may
we say, through decay—is full of abiding interest.

We know through the facts of our own individual experience something of the process of change. Our personal experience of the formation of our own religious conceptions helps us to understand the progress in natural sequence from the childly to the maturer faith, from the undefined belief in GOD, which is part of man's original equipment, to the belief in many gods of partial and different powers and then to the belief in One GOD. We have ourselves known corresponding stages in the realisation of our own Faith. And this progress, achieved at least in thought on a large scale by the noblest among Gentile teachers, is part of the ' testimony of the soul naturally Christian': the revelation of the soul's wants which the absolute religion must meet. This is one side of the great lessons of the Gentile religions; and on the other hand the popular corruptions of simple religions are no less instructive. In a different sense these also are witnessings of the soul to Christ, so far as they shew that man cannot live in the thin atmosphere of abstractions, but must make for himself objects to which he can approach and which, in a sense which he can realise, may go before him.

There is then we believe, to gather up what has been said, a certain original correspondence between national religions and national charac-

teristics. As each nation contributes something
to the fulness of the life of humanity, and something also to our knowledge of man's powers; even
so it is with the manifestation of their religious
beliefs and aspirations. In the earliest stage of
society perhaps the religion is the interpreter no
less than the bond of the nation. And even afterwards, in the later stages of natural progress or
degeneration, there are further lessons to be
learnt. There is also a law which connects the
successive phases of each popular religion in its
process of development or disintegration. In a
certain sense therefore we may speak of a historical science of religion as we speak of a
historical science of language. But the parallel
must not be pressed too far. Man contains within
himself all the springs from which speech flows.
Nothing is added which is not the consequence of
what precedes. The development of language
will consequently be continuous and everywhere
like in kind, if not like in form or in degree.
But in the case of religion it is not so. Our
knowledge of GOD depends, as we have seen,
upon the revelation which He is pleased to make
of Himself. And the natural voice of humanity
proclaims with no uncertain sound that He has
in fact made Himself known in various ways and
at various times. There is, no doubt, a close

relation between all alleged revelations and the
state of things in which they were brought forward. In the case of fictitious revelations it is
possible to find an explanation of their origin and
acceptance in the circumstances under which they
were received. In the revelations of which the
Bible is the record we maintain that such an
explanation is impossible. In this case there is
indeed a divine fitness which connects every
revelation of GOD with the circumstances under
which it is given; but the circumstances do not
produce, nor have they even a tendency to
produce, the revelation of which they are the
condition. The medium does not create the life.

It follows therefore that in the historical study
of religion we shall have two groups of facts to
coordinate and interpret, those which present the
evolution of the religious idea of man from within
according to the working of his own proper
powers; and those which represent the appropriation of super-added truths communicated
directly by GOD, not to all at once, but to a
representative people and to representative men.
We have to observe the history of religious ideas
in 'the nations' and in 'the people.' The two
streams perpetually intermix. The human often
opens the way for the divine, and provides the

channel in which it can best flow: the divine
adds to the human that towards which it tended
and which it could not supply.

A single illustration will bring out clearly
the distinction which I desire to draw. There
was, as has been already noticed, a preparedness,
so to speak, for the reception of the doctrine of
the unity of GOD among the Shemitic races.
The structure of their language and the tendency
of thought which it represented, qualified them
both to apprehend and to retain the truth. Nowhere else in the world can we find the same
ruling idea of symmetry, the same simplicity, the
same stationariness. Thus there was, it is true, a
divine congruity in the fact that Abraham—a
Shemite—became the Father of the faithful;
but as he stands out among idolatrous polytheists
of the same race we feel also that the possession
of the truth whereby he was a source of blessing
to all nations came from a Divine gift and not from
a natural 'instinct' shared by him with his fellow-
Shemites. The call of Abraham and his obedience
of faith is a fresh beginning in the religious life
of mankind, a true new creation. The later
history of the East is a signal commentary on this
central revelation to the world. The 'One GOD'
of Judaism, of Christianity, and of Mohammedanism is proclaimed to be 'the GOD of Abraham.'

There is, as has been often pointed out, no historic monotheism which does not start from this definite covenant which GOD made with him who still after nearly four thousand years is called in the land of his pilgrimage, the land of faith, 'the friend of God.'

But even when we have thus distinguished two streams of religious ideas, and claimed for special revelation, symbolised in the call of Abraham, its proper place in the religious history of the world, the part fulfilled by heathendom in the training of humanity for Christ—the broken imperfect representation of the normal discipline and development (so to speak) of the religious power in man as he was created—does not lose its importance. Two arguments will be sufficient to establish the point. The first is derived from the office which the two great types of the religious thought of the Aryan race actually discharged in the development of Judaism : the second lies in the direct words of the inspired writers.

No student of the history of Judaism can fail to recognise the lasting effects which Cyrus and Alexander—the representatives of the Eastern and Western Aryan civilizations—wrought upon the Jewish Church. The services which Persia rendered to the education of the world have descended to us through the influences of the later organisation of the people of Israel. The work of Greece, on the other hand, lives for the simplest Christian in the New Testament. It can hardly be presumptuous to say that without the discipline of the Persian supremacy and the quickening impulse of Greek thought, a medium could not have been prepared to receive and record the revelation of the Gospel. The chosen people gathered to itself in due time the treasures which other races had won.

Not to pursue this subject in detail, it will be enough for the student to compare the Jewish people before and after the Captivity to understand what they owed to Persian influence. Idolatry, which had been their besetting sin in earlier ages, disappeared. At the same time fuller views of the unseen world were opened before them. The kingdom became a church : an ecclesiastical system was consolidated : teachers stood by the side of priests : prayer assumed a new importance in worship : the bond of the society was felt more and more to be spiritual and not only local.

The conquests of Alexander and the consequent increase and wider extension of the Jews of 'the Dispersion' served to deepen this feeling of the potential universality of the Jewish revelation in its final completeness. Alexandria was added as a third centre of the faith to Jerusalem and Babylon. Greek thoughts were brought under the light of the concentrated belief in the unity of GOD and in His Personal sovereignty over creation. The Greek language was slowly adapted to the more exact and complete expression of the conceptions which Hebrew could only convey in a colossal outline. Let any one, to say all at once, compare the Greek Testament with the LXX. and with the Hebrew original, and he will be able to estimate the value of those instruments of precise analysis and exposition which the unconscious labours of the whole Greek race prepared for Christians from the first.

There are distinct, if scanty, acknowledgments of this world-wide fulfilment of the one counsel of GOD even in the Old Testament. In the patriarchal age Melchizedek is the symbol of the truth. And in two most remarkable passages of the book of Deuteronomy even alien and false worships are presented as part of the divine ordering of humanity. The Lord the GOD of Israel had 'divided all the host of heaven unto all the peoples under the whole heaven' (iv. 19). He had 'given them' to the nations but not to

His own people (xxix. 26). Even these idolatries
had a work to do for Him, an office in the
disciplining of men, however little we may be
able to understand the scope of its fulfilment.
The description which Isaiah gives of the work
of Cyrus 'the Lord's Shepherd' (xliv. 28), 'the
Lord's Anointed' (xlv. 1), is more familiar.

In the New Testament the conception of a
growth of humanity underlies in one sense the
whole picture of the age. The Gospel came at
'the fulness of time' (Gal. iv. 4; comp. Eph. i.
10; Tit. i. 3; Rom. v. 6), which answered alike to
the set period of the will of the Father, and to
the preparation of the many 'sons.' Such a view
of the absolute correspondence between the one
divine fact and the circumstances under which it
was wrought follows directly from the doctrine
of the age-long revelation of the Word, who was in
the world and (in another sense) was ever coming
into the world which He had made (John i. 9 ff.).
And the few notices which occur in the apostolic
writings of the position of the heathen towards
the Christian revelation take account equally of
what they had been able to do and of what they
had failed to do (Acts xiv. 17; xvii. 24 ff.; Rom.
i. 19 ff.). The words of the Lord are heard from
the beginning to the end *Other sheep I have which
are not of this fold* (John x. 16)—sheep who were

not the less sheep because they had not yet recognised their shepherd.

The truth which was thus realised in the
history of the Jews and recognised in the teaching of the New Testament found a partial exposition among some of the early Greek Fathers, of
whom Justin Martyr and Clement of Alexandria
are the best examples. These fathers and others,
particularly men of the Alexandrine School,
though they did not rise to the apprehension of
the special office of Gentile nations in the divine
economy, which a larger view of the relations of
the parts of our vast human life enables us to
gain, yet saw clearly that there was a work for and
of GOD going on during the apparent isolation of
the heathen from the region in which the Spirit
revealed Him. The teaching of Justin is singularly full of interest, and in some respects
unique. The truths in the utterances of heathen
philosophy and poetry are due, he says, to the
fact that 'a seed of the Word is implanted' (or
rather 'inborn,' ἔμφυτον) 'in every race of men.'
Those who grasped the truth lived 'according to
a part of the seminal Word' even as Christians
live 'according to the knowledge and contemplation of the whole Word, that is Christ.' They
'nobly uttered what they saw akin to the part

'of the divine seminal Word which they had
'received.' The opponents of Christianity pleaded
that it was of recent date, and that men who lived
before its promulgation were irresponsible. Justin
replies: 'he has been taught...that Christ is the
'first born (πρωτότοκον τοῦ Θεοῦ) of GOD, as being
'the Logos (Word, Reason), in which all the race
'of men partook. And those who lived with the
'Word (with Reason) are Christians even if they
'were accounted atheists, as, among Greeks, Socrates
'and Heraclitus and those like them, and among
'non-Greeks Abraham, and Ananias, Azarias and
'Misael, and Elias, and many others....'

But while Justin acknowledges in this way
that there were, in one sense, Christians before
Christ among the heathen and an actual working
of the Word through the reason of man, he in-
clines to the popular but untenable belief, which
had been long current at Alexandria, that the
Gentile teaching on 'the immortality of the soul,
'and punishments after death and the like' were
borrowed from the Jewish prophets[1].

Clement is equally undecided in his view of
the origin of the truths of heathendom. On the
whole he regards them as partly borrowed from

---

[1] Just. M. *Apol.* ii. 8 (p. 188 Otto); ii. 13 (p. 200); *Apol.* i.
46 (p. 110); i. 44 (p. 106). Comp. *Apol.* i. 5; ii. 10.

Jewish revelation and partly derived from reason illuminated by the Word—the final source of reason. There was, he says, in philosophy a little fire, stolen as it were by a Prometheus, fit to give light, if duly fanned: faint traces of wisdom and an impulse from GOD. And so Greek philosophers were in this sense thieves and robbers, who before the Lord's coming took from the Hebrew prophets fragments of truth. They did not possess the deeper knowledge of its import (οὐ κατ᾽ ἐπίγνωσιν) but appropriated what they took as their own doctrines. Some truths they disfigured: others they overlaid with restless and foolish speculations: others they discovered, for perhaps they also had he concludes 'a spirit of wisdom.'

Yet whatever might be the connexion between Jewish and Gentile doctrines, both systems were related to the Gospel as parts to the whole, and parts mutilated by the perverseness of men. The various schools of philosophy, Jewish and heathen alike, are described by Clement under a memorable image as rending in pieces the one Truth, as the Bacchanals rent the body of Pentheus and bore about the fragments in triumph. Each one, he says, boasts that the morsel which has fallen to it is all the Truth...Yet by the rising of the Light all things are brightened...and he continues, ' he that again combines the divided parts and

' unites the Word, the revelation, of GOD (λόγος) in
' a perfect whole, will, we may be assured, look
' upon the Truth without peril.'

But though Clement writes undecidedly as to
the final source of the truths in Greek philosophy
he expresses a definite judgment as to the office
which philosophy fulfilled for the Greeks, and
still in his time continued to fulfil, as a guide to
righteousness—a work of divine providence[1].

At the same time he limits the preparatory
work of heathendom to the teaching of philosophers and poets. It was natural that he should
do so. The classical religions of the Greeks and
Romans had no sacred books. The last word of
Greek religious thought was philosophy: the
last word of Roman religious thought was law.
Clement indeed was acquainted, at least by hear-
say, with the writings and speculations of the
Brahmans and of Zoroaster and of the Buddhists,
but they appeared to him simply as the works of
philosophers and not as the authoritative sources
of wide-spread religious belief[2]. The idea of a
heathen book-religion was wholly strange to him.

---

[1] Clem. Al. *Strom.* i. § 87, p. 369; i. § 57, p. 349. Comp.
Strom. i. § 18; § 28; vi. § 159; § 42; § 167; i. § 99; vi. §§ 44,
47 ff.

[2] *Strom.* i. § 68, p. 355; § 72, p. 360. Comp. iii. § 60, p. 538.
Strom. i. § 69, p. 357; § 133, p. 399; v. 104, p. 711.
Strom. i. § 71, p. 359. Lightfoot, *Colossians*, p. 155 note.

But for our purpose it will be best to confine our
attention to the old 'Book-religions.' There is
much of the deepest interest in the religious
beliefs of savages: much also in the religious
beliefs which are preserved in works of art; but
the actual records from which men drew and still
draw their faith are both more accessible and,
with every allowance for their obscurity, more
certain in their interpretation. A century ago
such an inquiry as is now open to the theological
student would have been impossible. As it is the
original writings of Confucianism, Brahmanism,
Buddhism, Zoroastrianism are rapidly being placed
before us in intelligible forms; and it can hardly
be an accident that each of the three great
families of speech offers collections of sacred books
which present in a form capable of a direct analysis
the faiths which correspond with them.

CHAPTER V.

WHAT then, we have now to ask, are the characteristic thoughts which underlie the præ-Christian Book-religions? and what lessons can we learn from them? These lessons, as we have already seen, will be twofold, according as they are drawn from the original conceptions to which the several religions bear witness, and from the subsequent embodiments of them. The original conceptions will serve at once to enlarge and to define our view of man's religious nature; and if so, to illuminate our own faith; for if Christianity be, as we believe, universal, then every genuine expression of human religious thought will enable us to see in the Gospel some corresponding truth which answers to it. If we can understand what whole races of men were feeling after, we shall have a clue to the discovery of mysteries for which we, with our limited religious instincts, should not otherwise have sought. And in the growing assurance that the Gospel meets each real need of humanity, we shall find the highest conceivable proof of its final and absolute truth.

This then is one end of our inquiry; and the other is to apprehend the fatal course of the actual history of primitive Gentile religions. For so much will be clear that in each case the central idea from which they all start, the need of a harmony between man and the world and GOD, after it had at first found a popular expression through the voice of great teachers, became as time went on, more and more overlaid on the one side by speculation and on the other side by ceremonialism. That which originally found spontaneous acceptance among different races as a religion became universally a philosophy or a ritual.

Something of the same twofold degeneration can be seen in the history of the Christian Faith, but the preservation in the Church of the original records of the historic revelation provides in this case an adequate outward test of all later developments and an effectual source of reformation.

All that will be said will necessarily require to be carefully verified, and completed by more

detailed inquiries. I can only hope that some
who have the leisure will follow out lines of
thought which seem to me to promise to this age
a manifestation of Truth fuller in its assurance
and more glorious in its promises than men have
yet received. We are placed in a position in
which it is first becoming possible to see that the
Gospel is the answer to every religious aspiration
and need of man and men. We must then, if we
are to comprehend its scope, strive to hear and to
understand every voice of those who have sought
GOD, even if they be only voices of 'children
crying in the dark.'

To this end we must endeavour to keep in
view the ruling thoughts of different systems;
and at the very outset of our inquiry we may, I
think, characterise by three words the three
groups of præ-Christian Book-religions—the Turanian, the Aryan, the Shemitic—and such a
characterisation will serve as a general clue to
guide us as we go farther. We may say with justice, speaking broadly, that the Chinese (Turanian)
religions are impressed with the stamp of order,
the Aryan with that of nature, the Shemitic with
that of history. So it is that the resemblances
between these three groups of religions are greatest in their earliest stages. Then the peculiar
influences of race begin to work; and their

original correspondences are slowly obliterated
by developments in these three directions.

(i) THE RELIGIONS OF CHINA.

The indigenous religious systems of China—
and here we must use the term religious in its
widest sense—are, I have said, impressed by the
conception of a supreme order. The two great
contemporary teachers, Lao-tzŭ and Confucius,
who lived in the sixth century B.C., took this
conception and gave it shape in converse and
complementary forms. Lao-tzŭ embodied it in a
system of mysticism, and Confucius in a system
of materialistic realism, or, in modern language,
of positivism.

With Lao-tzŭ the order—the 'way' (Tâo)—
pointed to absolute repose, so that the end of the
wise man was to strip off every personal thought
and want and joy and sorrow and yield himself to
the invisible law of his being. With Confucius
the visible order was the one sufficient sphere of
the citizen's activity. Man could, he taught,
find in himself the power to fulfil the perfect law,
and also find in the past the unchanging and
sufficient models for his action. In both cases
the order which the teacher aimed at realising
was something sovereign over the mutability of

physical nature and life. Both teachers again
regarded the earth as the one scene of human
interest. Both wished for a return to the old
paths. Both found their golden age in the past.
Evil without and within was treated by them as
something transitory and removable. Neither
looked to any future existence as an occasion for
just retribution; nor do they offer any direct
doctrine on another state.

But both Lao-tzŭ and Confucius seem to have
used many earlier thoughts, and there are striking
correspondences in their physical views which
probably represent the traditional opinions of
their time. And even more than this: Confucius
in spite of his practical bent, expresses now and
then thoughts which answer to the quietism of
Lao-tzŭ (*Analects* xv. 4; *Shŭ King* v. 3).

(a) *Traces of the primitive religion.*

It is still more important that Confucius
and Lao-tzŭ alike left much in the popular
beliefs and practices of their age unchanged and
untouched. All that is properly speaking theological in the national Chinese religion is older
than their teaching; and this primitive, præ-
Taouist, præ-Confucian religion, which survives

to the present time in great national ceremonies
and in domestic worship, offers many points of the
greatest interest. It has no priesthood, no mythology. The sacrifices which are offered represent
dependence on the power to which they are made
and gratitude for protection, but they include
no thought of expiation or propitiation; and no
essentially evil powers whose malevolence needs
to be averted are recognised in this earliest
faith. A fellowship between heaven and earth
is established through the spirits of the departed
which are placed in close connexion with the
celestial hosts in the most solemn acts of worship.

The Shû-King, in which the chief traces of the
primitive religion are preserved, gives a picture of
patriarchal faith and worship which is singularly
simple and reverent, nor is there any reason to
doubt that it represents what were commonly held
in the time of Confucius to have been the customs
and opinions in the days of the early kings.

The first account of sacrifice seems to carry
us beyond the limits of China. In this we are
brought into the presence of a majestic spiritual
hierarchy. The conception is essentially mono-
theistic and not polytheistic. Next to the Supreme Lord stands his foremost counsellors, to
whom is committed the care of elements or

provinces of life. At a greater distance are ranged vasts hosts of subordinate spirits to whom various ministries are assigned; and with these are associated spirits of the dead who in some cases are raised to be 'assessors of heaven.'

But while the conception of spiritual powers is pure and noble, the approach to them was not supposed to be open to all. The worship of the Supreme Lord (Shang-tî) has been confined in historic times to the Emperor, who appears before Him as the representative of the whole nation; and there is no evidence in the old books that He was ever worshipped directly by the people at large. Moreover a change in expression tended to obscure the distinctness of the early thought of the one Supreme Lord. Under the Chow dynasty the title 'Heaven and Earth' came to be used for the simple 'Heaven,' and the imperial sacrifices were said to be offered to 'Heaven and Earth.' Such language might easily give occasion for losing both the unity and the spirituality of the primitive faith; and this seems to have been in fact the case.

At the same time there are significant traces in the books of the Shû-King of a fuller expression of the religious consciousness than Confucius himself acknowledged. They recognise heavenly powers which freely sway the affairs of men by laws of right: the influence of the departed upon the affairs of earth: the action of what we can only regard as a personal Providence, whose counsel is executed by the earthly king.

The ceremonial institutions which were based upon these early beliefs have been continued to the present time, even if the beliefs themselves have lost much of their power. Two of these, the imperial worship of Shang-tî, and the general worship of ancestors, present most impressively, and as it were under the form of a primæval tradition, two conceptions which as yet we have not mastered in their Christian fulfilment, the solidarity and the continuity of the race. The Chinese are commonly held to be a prosaic people. They have at least preserved in these national customs a vivid expression of the most far-reaching fellowship of men in the present and through all time. In the one the nation is gathered up and finds unity in its head, and so appears before its unseen Lord: in the other the family is realised as one through all the stages of succession; and few thoughts are grander than that which holds that the achievements of a great man extend the privileges of his nobility to his ancestors (comp. Luke i. 72). It is no doubt true that the practical effects of these venerable observances fall far below their true conception. The text of the imperial prayers is not accessible. The solemnities of ancestral worship degenerate into forms. Still the institutions themselves have a meaning for us. They come to us as a message from a patriarchal age, declaring what man reaches out to and what by himself he cannot obtain. As we look on them with true human sympathy we seem to see a dim shadow of Melchizedek moving among his people.

These primitive religious conceptions form the background to the characteristic teaching of Laotzŭ and Confucius in which as we have seen the religious tendency of China towards order finds characteristic and complementary expression.

(b) *Taouism.*

The Tâo-tih King—the Book of Tâo and Virtue—represents an independent and characteristic form of speculation which constantly recurs in the spiritual history of men (Buddhism, Gnosticism, Quietism). There is no reason to think that the teaching was derived from any foreign source. The book—which is about twice as long as the Sermon on the Mount—recognises the old faith and specially the worship of ancestors; but it gives a philosophic view of being and not a religious system. The interpretation of the keyword Tâo is difficult and complex. Literally it means 'way,' and suggests that there is an archetypal idea of the whole sum of things and of each part (§ 39). It has no name (§§ 25, 32, 41). In itself it represents the indeterminate, the absolute, the unconditioned; in relation to things observed it is the law of being; in relation to action it is as conceived, the right way, and as realised, virtue. It has no beauty to look at but in use it is inexhaustible (§ 35).

The thought of Tâo defines the sense of unity in things which we feel directly and do not reach by reasoning (§ 62); and our business is to discern the relation of the world, life, conduct to Tâo, for the true order of things in space any time is through, according to, unto Tâo. Such a conception admits no reference to will or design : will implies resistance and design implies succession ; but Tâo *is*.

We can see the fulfilment of Tâo in 'Nature.' The elements and forces of 'Nature' fulfil their parts spontaneously, yielding themselves to an inspiring power (§§ 64, 29, 32, 37, 62). So for men and each man there is a true ruling idea to which perfect submission is due (comp. Hebr. vi. 1 φερώμεθα); but we are always substituting for this our own self-chosen aims and ways. The

wise man however has no private aim (§§ 13, 51,
77). He is empty (§§ 11, 15): he knows his
ignorance (§ 20): he does nothing (§§ 2, 29, 43,
56–7, 63): he is free in the sense that (as the
stone falls) he fulfils the law of his being. Perfect
freedom is, he knows, identical with perfect obedience. He will not strive (§§ 66, 68, 73). His
strength is in humility (§§ 8, 9, 22). He becomes
a little child (§§ 10, 28). But while the effects
of all violence (as war, conquest, capital punishment) are transitory (§ 23), there is strength in
weakness (§§ 76, 78). Hence it follows that the
results of artificial progress—material and intellectual—are full of peril (§§ 3, 12, 80; 48, 65, 71);
and through this comes at last the fall of states
(§§ 17, 18).

Such a system contained no Gospel for the
poor. It appealed to the self-reliance of the
solitary thinker. At the same time its insistence
on the existence of one essence in all things (§ 28),
and on the permanence and safety of the sage
(§ 50) gave occasion to the acceptance and development of gross superstitions in regard to charms
and divinations, so that at present Taouism is in
China the most debased type of religion, though
it is said to have retained more of its original
form in Corea. It is difficult to trace the history
of its decline, which offers striking resemblances

to that of Neo-Platonism. This was largely influenced by the permanent introduction of Buddhism into China in the first century (A.D. 65). Lao-tzŭ was assimilated to Buddha. Images were made of three Taouist Holy Ones. The doctrine of future punishment became a powerful engine in the hands of the priests. Ancestral worship was no longer a fellowship of the family, but a service of fear for the averting of evil. Subordinate Gods were multiplied as representatives of the powers of nature and charged with the interests of human life. Even within the last half century the God of war (Kwan-tî) has been made equal to Confucius. And though these are not properly Taouist deities their temples are in charge of Taouist priests.

While this practical degeneration of Taouism as a religious system proceeded, the moral teaching of Taouism still retained wide influence ; and ' The book of rewards and punishments,' a collection of moral aphorisms of great beauty, is said to be at present the most popular religious book in China.

(c) *Confucianism.*

The system of Lao-tzŭ, though it was a necessary philosophical embodiment of the fundamental Chinese conception of an absolute order of

things, was alien from the practical character of
the people. So far as it obtained acceptance, it
was with select thinkers as a speculative system
or with the mass of people as a system of
magical powers. The latter aspect is, as we have
seen, that which has been most permanent. It
was supposed that the wise man obtained command over the spirits of earth and heaven by
which he was surrounded, and in virtue of this
imaginary power of its priests Taouism still
maintains its hold on China. The system of
Confucius however is the most complete expression of the national character. Confucius is
the only statesman who has fashioned a 'religion'; and he sought it in the establishment
of an earthly order. He declined to entertain
the questions, Whence? Whither? The life of
this world was, he held, sufficient to occupy men.
'Ke Loo asked about serving the spirits of the
'dead. The Master said: While you are not able
'to serve men, how can you serve their spirits?
'Ke Loo added: I venture to ask about Death.
'He was answered: While you do not know life,
'how can you know about death?' (*Analects* xi. 11).
So 'there were four things which the Master
'taught, letters, ethics, devotion of soul, truthful-
'ness' (*id.* 24). Through these he endeavoured
to shape an external order which should at once

develop and restrain human powers; and he held
that perfect virtue consists in the manifestation
of 'gravity, generosity of soul, sincerity, earnest-
'ness and kindness' (*Analects* xvii. 6).

The foundation of the system of Confucius lay
in the assumption, of which there were traces in
the older writings, that man is born good, 'born
'for righteousness' (*Analects* vi. 17; cf. *Mencius*
vii. 1, 15; vi. (1), 2, 1 f.). 'The great man,' said
Mencius, who was the victorious apostle of Confucianism, 'is he who does not lose his childs-
'heart' (iv. 2, 13); and while he recognised the
complexity of the constitution of man, he affirmed
that man was capable of recognising a sovereign
law within. To follow this and not some chance
impulse is, he shews with a vigour and decision
not unworthy of Butler, to follow Nature (vii.
1, 17). In this sense 'benevolence is man' (vii.
2, 16); and the highest is within the reach of
all.

At the same time both Confucius and Mencius
recognised that men are liable to go astray under
the influence of circumstances. They have need
therefore of learning the lesson of past experience
(*Analects* xv. 30), and of submitting to discipline
and government. Hence followed the paramount

importance attached by Confucianists to education and the ceremonial of life; and it would be difficult to find anywhere a more harmonious view of the whole ordering of conduct in the state and in the family and in personal intercourse than that which is given in the *Lî Kî* ('A collection of the Rules of Propriety or Ceremonial Usages'). It is easy to disparage the observances as simply formal and external, but they witness to the intimate relation of the outward to the inward, and foreshadow in some sense the sacramental aspects of the world and life which Christianity has revealed. In a most pregnant saying, Confucius shewed that he looked beyond the impressions of sense. 'The Master 'said: "It is according to the rules of propriety" 'they say; "It is according to the rules of 'propriety" they say. Are gems and silk all that 'is meant by propriety? "It is Music" they say; '"It is Music" they say. Are bells and drums all 'that is meant by Music?' (*Analects* xvii. 11.)

The regulation of life was indeed designed to express justly 'the five relations,' between parent and child, ruler and ruled, brethren, husband and wife, friends, which, as they underlie all society, must be duly regarded for the maintenance of the well-being of a state. 'The classic

' of Filial piety' (*Hsiâo King* : S. B. E. iii. 465–488)
describes in a short compass and in a most
impressive form the foundation of Chinese life.
' The services of love and reverence to parents
' when alive, and those of grief and sorrow to
' them when dead :—these completely discharge
' the fundamental duty of living men' (c. xviii.).
In a wider sense 'Filial piety commences with
' the service of parents; it proceeds to the service
' of the ruler; it is completed by the establishment
' of the character' (c. i.). For in spirit Filial piety
was held to extend to all the duties of life; and,
more than this, it is in essence 'the constant
' method of Heaven, the righteousness of Earth and
' the practical duty of Man,' the comprehensive law
of all being. Thus Chinese Society was organised
on a principle of absolute dependence. Since the
child, the citizen, owes everything to the past, he
renders to the past in acknowledgement of the
debt, and to the elder as representing it, complete
obedience. 'The Master said: I am not one
' who was born in the possession of knowledge : I
' am one who is fond of antiquity and earnest in
' seeking it there' (*Analects* vii. 19). The result
has been stability and stationariness.

Confucius, like Lao-tzŭ, left the old religion
undisturbed. He himself carefully observed the

customary rites with devout reverence. 'He 'sacrificed to the dead, as if they were present. 'He sacrificed to the spirits as if they were 'present' (*Analects* iii. 12). But life in harmony with the order of the world seemed to him to be the highest worship. 'The Master being very 'sick, Tsze-loo asked leave to pray for him...The 'Master said "My praying has been for a long 'time"' (*Analects* vii. 34). So it naturally followed that the observances of worship under Confucianism came to be official and representative, a part of the life of the state and not the satisfaction of personal wants. There was no appointed ministry: the head of each section of society performed the services by an inherent right. The old was left, but Confucius when pressed by his disciples to deal with spiritual subjects, justified his silence by the silence above. 'Tsze-kung 'said: If you, Master, do not speak, what shall we 'your disciples have to record? The Master said: 'Does Heaven speak? The four seasons pursue 'their courses, and all things are being continually 'produced, but does Heaven say anything?' (*Analects* xvii. 19; contrast Ps. xix.). But in the older books there is a recognition of providential government. The course of the seasons is supposed to shew God (*Yih King*, App. v. 8, 9: S. B. E. xvi.). And though the 'Heaven' of the primitive belief became in the teaching of Confucius the symbol of a stern, inexorable law, an order not made by man but recognised by him, yet in one passage of the Analects there is a pathetic appeal to 'Heaven' as having feeling with men. 'The 'Master said: Alas, there is no one that knows 'me...I do not murmur against Heaven. I do 'not grumble against men. My studies lie low, 'and my penetration rises high. But there is 'Heaven:—that knows me' (*Analects* xiv. 37).

It follows from what has been said that Confucianism offered no definite teaching on a future life. The opinions on this subject which have found currency in China have been due either to the original faith or to Buddhism. There was from early times a vague belief in the separation of two 'souls' at death: the animal soul descended to the earth and perished, while the 'spirit' was 'displayed on high in a condition 'of glorious brightness' (*Lî Kî*, xxi. 2). The great and the noble were supposed to enjoy heavenly felicity, and an early king is represented as speaking of his ancestors as 'spiritual sovereigns' (*Shû King*, vii. 2). But there is no evidence that this hope of happiness was for all. On the other hand there is no doctrine of punishment after death. It was held that retribution was exacted in the life of earth either from the offender himself, or from his descendants afterwards. 'The family that accumulates goodness is sure to 'have superabundant happiness; and the family 'that accumulates evil is sure to have super- 'abundant misery. The murder of a ruler by his 'minister, or of a father by his son, is not the 'result of the events of one morning, or one 'evening' (*Yih King,* App. iv. ii. § 5 : S. B. E. xvi. pp. 419 f.).

The history of China is the best comment on the strength and on the weakness of this most wonderful system of secularism leavened by the remains of a patriarchal faith. The Empire has been at once the most lasting in the world, and the most unprogressive. It has been lasting because it was the resolute expression of faith in a supreme and beneficent order, as against the pessimism of Hinduism and Buddhism which sees in the world of sense illusion and evil, and the endless conflict of popular Zoroastrianism. It has been unprogressive because Confucianism obscured the fact of sin, and substituted a morality for a theology, rules for a divine fellow-ship, obedience to a code for devotion to a living Lord, teaching for a Teacher—as many at the present day seem to believe that the Sermon on the Mount can take the place of the Risen Christ—

and adopted a type of order which was earthly
and human, of the world and not above it. In
China we see realised the effects of an absolute
law, obeyed apart from reference to an absolute
Lawgiver, of a personal moral discipline ruled by
the motive of self-regarding culture and not of
self-sacrifice. China has been able to conquer its
conquerors but not to inspire them; to make
them like itself but not to call out the fulness of
their life. The Chinese became what we may
suppose the Jews would have become if the
covenant with Abraham had not underlain the
Law.

Man's own nature was held to be the one
revelation of heaven (*Menc.* vii. (1), i.). This had
been perfectly embodied in a kingdom of earth in
the past, and the past became at once the rule
and the type for all time. There was therefore
no infinite ideal offered for the inspiration of
men, growing with their growth: no living connexion with GOD making Himself known according to the development of human powers. All
that could be had already been, so that hope
was limited to the expectation of a limited
cycle of change.

But, not to close with the sad side of the
picture, we may remember, as has been already

pointed out, that Confucius acknowledged the relation of Fatherhood as the basis of human life. So far he was on the way to hear the fulness of the Divine message to humanity. He saw that the father was the living lord of the family: that the Emperor was the father of the nation. His facts carried him no farther, and he shrank from adventurous if splendid guesses. Yet we can see that the revelation of a true Divine Father in the Mission of Christ completes what he began, and that his view of society illustrates the doctrine of the Fatherhood of GOD, and the brotherhood of men.

Under this aspect the indigenous faiths of China deserve far more careful study than they have received. They express to us with a voice clear independent and impressive some of the earliest beliefs of men. We can see in them as a power still living that which can be recognised in other religions in a distorted and exaggerated shape. Above all they present with unique force thoughts which at the present time seem to be essential for the interpretation of the Gospel to our own age, the solidarity of peoples and, in the end, of mankind, and the continuity of personal life in the family. These thoughts, as we have already seen, are embodied in the Im-

perial Sacrifices and in the worship of ancestors.
And as a primitive witness to the instincts or
aspirations of the human soul they turn our
attention to Christian teachings which have been
overlooked. For there is nothing which gave
strength to China which does not find a fitting
place in the Apostolic doctrine, while the Christian Faith guards against the evils which weak-
ened the Empire. The thought of continuity
finds complete expression in the promise 'to
'Abraham and his seed,' 'of whom was Christ as
'concerning the flesh.' The thought of solidarity
is hallowed in the conception of the Body of
Christ, in which Christians are 'members one
'of another.' The thought of totality is confirmed
in the fact that He is heir of all things through
Whom all things were made, and in Whom they
are destined to reach their consummation. The
thoughts are given to us in the Gospel and they
are all quickened by a continuous movement as
the revelation of GOD in men in humanity and in
the world is read more intelligently. Thus the
characteristic conceptions of China become a great
prophecy, and bear witness to a hope which will
not for ever be unsatisfied.

(ii) RELIGIONS OF INDIA.

The transition from China to India is the

transition from a region of prose to a region of poetry, from common sense to imagination : from life regarded as the expression of a fixed law to life regarded as the manifestation of innumerable separate forces, separate at least for man.

(a)   Hinduism.

The simplest form of Indian belief, and probably the simplest form of Aryan belief, that which is reflected in the oldest Vedic Hymns, is widely different from the Brahmanic and popular beliefs of India. It must not however be supposed that these Hymns represent a wide-spread, popular faith. They are rather the expression of personal, and in some respects, of conflicting opinions. The ideas of incarnation and transmigration and caste find no place in them. But they present in a vivid form the great truth that man stands in a close relation to nature in all its varying forms, as the expression of some unseen power. He is, in a certain sense, dependent on the sun and sky and storms and dawn. He may acknowledge an ever-present, immutable law : . but he acknowledges also vital relationships existing between outward things one to another and to himself which admit of infinite modifications. The conception of the Chinese Heaven

(Tien) as a constant order, and the conception of the Vedic Heaven (Varuna) as an approachable GOD, lie deep in human nature. In their simplest forms they are complementary and not contradictory aspects of being. We can set over against one another the confession of Lao-tzŭ and the great Hymn to Varuna, and feel that there is a partial truth in both : perhaps we can feel the partial truths more keenly when they are thus presented to us separately.

This then appears to be the characteristic of the Vedic Theology, that the great forces of nature Indra (the watery atmosphere), Surya (the sun), Agni (fire) and Ushas (the dawn) and the like represent personal action, though they are not personified. They are not Gods severally, but manifestations of GOD. There is no individuality, no subordination among them, and there is no trace of idolatry in the service through which they are approached. The worshipper turns from one title to another without defining in any way the great Being which lies behind and beyond all titles. He asks for specific, and in most cases, for material blessings. At the same time there are not unfrequent acknowledgments of sin, though sin is not apprehended in its depth, and prayers for forgiveness ;

and over all stands the belief in immortality and retribution. There are no temples, no priests, no ritual. We listen to profound childlike utterances of an awakened consciousness. The 'seers' who clothe the truths to which their eyes are opened write spontaneously. They must sing, even as the bird must sing. They give witness to a feeling which has not been confined in any specific form of service.

The weakness of such a system—if indeed it can be called a system—is obvious. Indeed, as has been already said, there is no reason to think that the Hymns answer to any general or widespread or popular belief. A belief of this kind is in a perpetual flux. It takes its impress from the emotions of individual teachers, and is for a time capable of moulding small groups of men; but, when it has once passed out of its first stage, it is unfitted for a national faith. The Vedic belief consequently was humanised, so to speak, defined, embodied in a ritual; and this new belief, Brahmanism, was interpreted in a philosophic theory and made the basis of a social organisation. Priests, warriors, citizens had their functions distinguished as the original Aryan race advanced in India by conquest.

In order to understand how this came to pass we must go back to the earliest Vedic Hymns.

It has been already noticed that in these Hymns the Divine names are names and do not answer to individualised deities. Each name represents for the time the whole Being of GOD so far as He is apprehended by the poet or the worshipper. This mysterious Being however is wholly undefined, and does not, except in the exertion of power, form an object of thought in the typical Vedic Theology.

But after a time the idea of an infinite, impersonal, ineffable existence, the source of all things and the support of all things, the neuter Brahma, was shaped, which thenceforward was taken as the basis of the Brahmanic faith. The origin of the word seems to be at present uncertain; the conception, however, is clear and consistent, and it is summed up in the statement that of Brahma and of Brahma alone this can be said, and this only, '*It is.*'

Two deductions follow at once from such a conception of the absolute foundation of religious belief. All things have come into being from Brahma, and there is in Brahma a unity of all things. That which distracts us in the appearance of things is Mayà—illusion. We gain in

other words in Brahmanism the notions of a
beginning of finite existence and of the coherence
of things, seen and unseen, which were wanting in
the Chinese conception of an eternal order and
undeveloped in Vedic theology. Out of these
two notions, which may be generally characterised
by the terms emanation and dependence, most
variously realised, later Indian systems have been
constructed. So far as they were embodied in
the proper Hindu beliefs, they present three chief
topics for our consideration, the doctrine of the
Deity, the doctrine of society, and the doctrine of
the final issue of things, on which we must touch
in succession.

The first step in the development of the
doctrine of Absolute Being, of Deity, was the
passage from the neuter Brahma to the masculine
Brahmâ, from the conception of a source of being
to that of a personal creator. But this word
'creator' must not mislead us. Creation is not
in the Indian belief an act of sovereign will, but,
so to speak, a necessity of the desire of Brahmâ.
The world is regarded on this theory as the
thought of Brahmâ veiled in material and illusory
forms. So far as it *is* it is coessential with him,
and will in the end be reabsorbed into him.

From the doctrine of the Deity we pass on to the doctrine of society.   Here again we must go back to the elementary thought of Brahmanism.   All finite being proceeds from (the neuter) Brahma.   This was the general principle which the religious statesman had to embody in a practical shape.   How could he reconcile it with the manifest differences in spiritual and moral and material capacities in men, even if he went no farther?   How could he maintain the divine affinity of mankind and yet recognise the degradation of individual men?   The answer to these questions was given in the theoretical organisation of the institution of caste. By that institution it was affirmed that all men, or rather all Hindus, for the Brahmanic horizon extends no further, are indeed sprung from Brahma (Brahmâ), but that they are differently related to him.   If he be represented as a man the Brahmans sprang from his face: the Kshattriyas from his shoulders, the Vaisyas from his thighs, the Sudras from his feet.   The meaning of the myth is obvious: divine energy whether in thought, or in courageous self-sacrificing service, or in commercial enterprise, or in menial duty, alike draws its strength directly from the Supreme Being, but it is by the highest energy

alone, by thought, that the connexion of man
with GOD is fully realised.

There cannot, I think, be any doubt that this
is the true moral conception of the theory of
caste. It is the enunciation of a divine unity in
an actual subordination. It presents an order
based upon the interpretation of the facts of life,
and not an order, like the Chinese, sovereign over
them. It does not concern us to inquire how the
actual institution of caste came into being in the
first instance: how far the distinction of the first
three castes, marked by the sacred thread, as
twice-born, represents the relation of conquerors
to the Sudras, the conquered: how far Hindu
society was ever divided into the 'four horizontal
strata' indicated by the traditional division: how
the 'warriors' and even the 'traders' were practically destroyed: how the theory of caste came
to be worked out in detail: how the separations
of caste were indefinitely multiplied and deepened.
The two great religious intuitions to which caste
bears witness, even in its last degradation, are
these, that there is on the one hand a Divine
element in humanity, and that this is realised
by a spiritual fellowship; and on the other that
society is based upon an organisation of unequal
and distinct functions. These principles have
been distorted and petrified by political and

priestly tyranny; but still they have given permanence to Indian life, and they have maintained
an independent spiritual power in the face of
dominant tyranny.

At first sight the idea of caste appears to fix
a definite limit to the range of Hinduism. But
taken in connexion with the popular development
of the conception of the Divine manifestation it
became a powerful aid to its propagation. Caste
is the outward expression of the belief that every
detail of life is religious. All that is characteristic
of an occupation is in a certain sense of Divine
appointment and under Divine sanction, and
therefore in its nature unchangeable. When, then,
the belief in transitory incarnations of the Divine
gained currency, it only became necessary to
recognise in a local deity an incarnation (in some
practical degree) of a Hindu deity, and to accept
the service of a Brahman for his worship, in order
to obtain in turn the elevation of the local
customs to the dignity of marks of a new caste
within the pale of the old religion.

The historical existence and prevalence of
caste has exerted in India a profound reflex
action upon the popular views of the conduct
of life generally which caste itself partially

defined. If outward circumstances were admitted to influence almost indefinitely the present
spiritual character of a man, it was natural that
an absolute value should be given to outward
religious observances. The act in each case
might be supposed to carry with it necessary
and unchangeable consequences. The whole
system of Hindu worship and Hindu asceticism
is based upon this theory. As a consequence, for
example, sacrifices in the later Hindu theory are
invested with a fixed and graduated value wholly
independent of the moral intention and character
of the offerer. Penances again are supposed to
bring a direct equivalent of divine reward. Worship in a word in all its forms is reduced to a
series of external performances essentially distinct
from morality. It is unnecessary to dwell on the
inevitable consequences of this corruption of the
duty of religious service. Yet two indirect results
of the popular belief deserve to be noticed. In
the first place the belief has served in part to
mitigate the evils of caste, and left open for all a
way, however narrow, to heaven. Thus in the
orders of Hindu devotees, or at least in some orders,
as in early Buddhism on a large scale, the distinc-
tions of caste are done away. On the other hand
the same belief has extinguished gratitude. He
who receives an act of kindness is reckoned to

confer a benefit upon the doer, because he has given him an opportunity of establishing a claim on heaven.

The theory of caste, which gives in some sense a Divine significance to the present order in which we live, raises questions at the same time as to the past and the future. How can we account for the startling differences which we recognise, and what will be their final issue? The answers to these questions were found by a recurrence to the fundamental doctrine of being and appearance. All that truly *is*, is in the theoretic Hindu faith, divine: all transitory appearances of things, all that falls under the senses, is a mere illusion, due to the selfwill of finite creatures. The happy end of the world will therefore be gained when each existence has cast off the cloak of vanity in which it has become enveloped. To this end souls are invested, from life to life, with material forms, as with prison-houses, in which they may be cleansed from the effects of the dimly-conceived declension from their original purity. The outward difference between man and brute and reptile image to the Hindu the inward differences of the souls which animate them. Hence all living creatures are looked upon as shewing stages in the purification of finite being. According to the nature of each life spent on earth the soul is supposed to receive after death an appropriate body for its next stage of existence. The myths of Plato will shew us how great an attraction this doctrine of transmigration exerts upon the imagination of men. At present I wish only to notice its general significance as an expression of an elementary religious consciousness. So far it seems to bear testimony to two great beliefs. It affirms the vital connexion of all the forms of animated being. It affirms a possible, if indefinitely distant, reunion of every isolated existence with the one absolute existence.

While these thoughts were taking shape, the popular theology was modified by corresponding changes. The Brahmanic conception of the Divine Being has risen before the minds of men in every age, but it cannot provide a resting-place for practical belief. We necessarily consider not only the origin of things, but also the actual constitution of things, the manifestations of Divine power. Hence the Indian mind found no rest in the abstract idea of the unity of Brahmâ. The various divine workings were gathered up by the Brahmanic teachers under their contrasted aspects of preservation and destruction; and these were assigned to distinct persons. Vishnu was the representative of the Divine Being as a Preserver,

Siva the representative of the Divine Being as a
Destroyer. And these three, Brahmâ, Vishnu and
Siva, were regarded in the age of the epic poems
as constituting a Trinity, *Trimurti*, three forms.
As such however they were considered to be not
three distinct beings, but three manifestations of
one Being. Now one name and now the other
was taken as the name of the One. 'Some
'worship Brahmâ,' it is said in one of the Puranas,
'others Vishnu, others Siva, but Vishnu, one yet
'threefold, creates, preserves, destroys; therefore
'let the pious make no difference between them.'
Elsewhere each of the three is represented as
subordinate to and even created by the One
ineffable Supreme Being, the Great Soul, lest the
conception of the Divine unity should be injured.
So great thinkers argued : meanwhile Brahmâ, the
Creator, the absolute God, almost passed out of
the mind of the people. 'It is doubtful if he was
'ever worshipped, though the *Brahma Purana*
'speaks of his being adored at Pushkara near
'Ajmer, and it is said that he still receives
'some worship there.' The thoughts of struggling,
suffering men were concentrated upon the deities
of preservation and destruction, or Vishnu and
Siva. And even these broad aspects of divine
working failed to meet the actual wants of
worshippers. These generalised deities were again

broken up into countless fragmentary powers, to whom some one portion or other of good or evil activity was assigned, and the Hindu pantheon was peopled as the old faith spread southward into the plains of Bengal, and came into contact with aboriginal creeds.

This multiplication of deities, or divine manifestations, springs out of and perpetuates one of the original characteristics of the earliest belief. In some regions of India, it has been said, ' every ' brook, every grove, every jutting rock has its ' divinity ; ' ' every institution, every pursuit, every ' power beneficent or maleficent is consecrated by ' a supernatural influence or presidency.' With these subordinate gods and popular beliefs of the ' Puranic ' age, we have at present no concern, except so far as they witness to the impulse which drives men at all times to the specialities of saint-worship, to characterise the impulse by its noblest type; but there is one feature of the greatest interest in the general mode of representing the beneficent action of Vishnu which cannot be passed over. Vishnu, the Preserver, is described as coming among his creatures in Avataras—Descents or Incarnations, both for purposes of judgement and redemption. These Avataras are variously reckoned, but most commonly they are said to be ten, of which the tenth is yet future. In each of the nine past Avataras Vishnu is said to have descended 'in a 'small portion of his essence,' taking the form of a fish, or a tortoise, or a boar, or a man-lion, or a dwarf, or a man, as the case might be. But most conspicuous among them is the Krishna-Avatara, in which Vishnu is said to have appeared in the form of a popular hero, Krishna. This legend of Krishna appears to have taken full shape first in the Bhagavad-Gita, an episode of the Mahabharata, and that possibly under Christian influences. None of its characteristic elements can be shewn to be earlier than the Christian era, and it has been argued from minute coincidences in detail that the framers of the story were not unacquainted with the Gospels. This is, however, very uncertain, and it must be enough to say that the idea of the Krishna-Avatara, in its most complete form, when divested of every unholy accessory, is essentially distinct from the Christian idea of the Incarnation. The assumption of humanity by Vishnu is in appearance only, and the human nature is wholly laid aside when Krishna, slain by a random shot of the hunter Jará (that is decay, old age), returns to the Great Being. Yet even so Krishnaism has been the strength of Hinduism. Again and again the belief in the most human manifestation of the Deity among his creatures which Hinduism ever fashioned has restored life and energy to the exhausted faith of the people.

Simultaneously with the growth of the popular faith, which naturally centred more and more in the fulfilment of ritual, two great philosophical schools arose, one of which professed to express the true end of the Vedas (Vedanta), and the other to unfold a rational system (Sankhya = number or reason). It would be useless for our purpose to endeavour to discuss their teaching, for they were the profound speculations of the few, and both left the system of caste undisturbed. But the fact of their existence must be recognised. They stand over against the declining polytheism like the systems of Plato and Aristotle, witnesses for the loftier strivings and the sad hopelessness of men. And while these rival philosophies took no account of social disorders and social reformation, they shewed on the side of speculation the action of those tendencies which found expression in the great popular movement of Buddhism. This movement we must now notice.

(b)　*Buddhism.*

To place Buddhism in its true position we

must recall the characteristic type of the Aryan religions. They all bear, as has been said, the stamp of Nature. But Nature may be found either outside us or within us: it may be taken to be the sum of the facts of the external world, or, the sum of the facts which belong to man's consciousness. Hinduism, in spite of its lofty aspirations and in spite of its speculative protests, fell completely as a popular religious system under the dominion of the material order. Social subordination became an organised slavery. Devotion became formalism. The conception of the manifoldness of the Divine working in the world became abject and degrading polytheism.

It is probable that the tendencies to these conceptions were already clearly marked when the Buddhist reform was set on foot. The date of its author, Gautama, known also as Sakya-Muni (the Sakya sage), Siddhartha (he who has accomplished his aim), is uncertain. He is commonly placed in the 6th or 5th century B.C. He was a prince of the warrior (Kshattriya) caste, and his aim was generally to organise and embody the noblest ideas of the Hindu faith. He was himself treated in later Hinduism as an Avatara of Vishnu; and many of his chief disciples were Brahmans. The bitter antagonism between Brahmanism and Buddhism did not begin for some centuries after Gautama's death. It is true that the essential differences between the two systems existed from the first; but at the beginning Gautama probably regarded himself as the right interpreter of the spirit of the faith which he inherited.

According to the teaching of the well-known legend Gautama was moved by the spectacle of the common sorrows of humanity, age and disease and death, to give up his wealth and place in order that he might seek a mode of deliverance for men. This he seemed to find within himself, not in the teaching of outward things but in intelligence, the teaching of his own nature. Such a conception had a starting-point in earlier thought. The world was represented by some Hindu philosophers as the thought of the Absolute Being. By thought then, Gautama argued, we can rise, on our part, to the true knowledge of Being, a knowledge which will bring perfect rest.

This conclusion was not reached however without severe struggles. Gautama at first sought peace in the way of severest penance and self-mortification. For six years he pursued this discipline with pitiless resolve, but he gained fame only and not the rest for which he sought.

Conscious of failure he gave up his severities and fasting, and was himself forsaken by his disciples. Then followed his temptation under the sacred Bo-tree; and after a fierce struggle he seemed to be answered that absolute peace was attainable by inward culture of the heart and love to others, resting on the true understanding of things.

The doctrine of right intelligence as the one supreme guide and end of life carried with it essentially the complete overthrow of what we have seen to be the characteristics of the later Brahmanic system. It overthrew caste so far as it was supposed to represent an actual spiritual inequality in men. It overthrew the whole system of external worship so far as it was supposed to have in itself an objective value. For caste it substituted the idea of universal brotherhood. For worship it substituted the idea of personal service. Hinduism fell of necessity till it came to be worship without morality. Buddhism started with being morality without worship; and it is as a system of morality, but of morality as being of inherent obligation, that Buddhism claims to be reckoned among the religions of the world. In this respect it is among the noblest as it is the vastest moral spectacle in history.

It offers a Law, a Law of the Gentiles, which is
indeed a prophecy. For if we regard the theory
of Buddhism as a whole we cannot represent it
better than by saying that it is from first to last
the embodiment of self-sacrifice. Self-sacrifice is
the key to the law of Buddhism, and, as far as I
can see, self-sacrifice is the true explanation of
its last hope, Nirvâna. Such a fact is full of encouragement for the Christian teacher; for it is
in virtue of this doctrine of sacrifice that Buddhism
has won its way to be, perhaps, the most wide-
spread religion in the world. The doctrine may
have been defaced and veiled, yet it has never
been wholly hidden; and in this religion of pure
intelligence we have the testimony of about a
third of the human race to the natural strivings
of man towards a pure ideal which he cannot
reach.

Self-sacrifice is the central thought of Buddhism. We shall now notice shortly how the idea
was gained and how it was applied. The necessity
of sacrifice followed directly from the Buddhist
view of finite existence. Buddhism does not
concern itself specially with the origin of things.
Its general view of the material universe as a
visible system is borrowed from Hinduism, and

has no features of peculiar interest. Its interest lies in the interpretation of transitory being. It looks on life as it is and seeks to bring it to its proper issue. The most universal fact in life is pain, and from this fact of pain Gautama started. What is the origin of pain? Can it be prevented? and if so, How can it be prevented? In answering these questions Gautama regarded man only so far as he falls within the range of our present observation. The various bodily and mental powers with which the individual is endowed are gathered into four groups (skandhas), and it is shewn that all these are transitory. Nothing is said of that which may underlie them. In other words, Gautama looked upon man as entangled in a pitiable existence and inquired what hope there might be of his deliverance. Following the lessons of his own experience he gave his conclusions in the 'four sublime truths' which constitute the primitive and cardinal elements of the Buddhist Creed. These deal with Pain and its cause, the end of Pain, and the Path to gain the end:

1.   Pain lies ultimately in finite existence.

2.   Pain is the necessary consequence of preceding causes which give rise to desire.

3.   An end can be put to pain by extinguishing all desire.

4. This end cån be secured by the way which the Buddha taught.

This way, as we have seen, is the way of knowledge. So far as a man looks at things in their infinite relations he loosens the chain which binds him to the phantom of personal being. True knowledge in a word kills desire by absolute repose; and such knowledge is essentially un-selfish. It lifts a man out of self; and he who is on the way to knowledge will necessarily both curb his own wishes and seek to help forward others along the path to rest which he has found. Just as ignorance is the spring and support of self-assertion and selfishness, so knowledge includes the idea of sacrifice, the giving up of all that belongs to man as individual. The thought is on one side not unlike that of Socrates when he said that unrighteousness is ignorance; but the Buddhist doctrine seems to be nobler than the Greek, inasmuch as the knowledge of the Buddhists is inherently of a social value. And it is worthy of remark that in the original records of Buddhism there is a word (*maitri*) which is commensurate with *charity*, Christian love (ἀγάπη).

Gautama extended this obligation of tenderness towards others to man's relations to all sentient beings; and this characteristic teaching was deepened by the doctrine of transmigration which he borrowed from Hinduism in a modified form. For the true Buddhist does not acknowledge the permanence of any individual soul which passes from life to life. He holds that the continuity of being is maintained in another way. Each man at his death is supposed to leave behind him the whole moral sum of his actions (*karma*, doing). By this a spiritual heir, so to speak, is called into existence, to whom falls the full inheritance of the good or evil desert which the original doer had accumulated. This embodiment of the issues of the past life in a new and corresponding life is the essential element in the Buddhist belief in successive births; and it is no less fitted than the simple doctrine of transmigration to keep alive the feeling of a common relationship between the believer and all animated beings.

As a consequence of this connexion of life, based upon a moral foundation, it has been held by the great Buddhist teachers that there is a true solidarity of life, that the whole condition and fate of the world, its cycles of destruction and reconstruction, depend upon the sum of merit and demerit gathered by separate beings. Every action therefore has, on this theory, a social value.

To know this is to find an object of endeavour, and since love is the direct offspring of intelligence : or, to express the same truth otherwise, since knowledge claims sacrifice: the highest in the Buddhist calendar of saints is the man who seeks knowledge and the end of knowledge not only for himself but also for others : who is prepared to defer his own attainment of the goal if he can guide others towards it.   It was in this spirit that the prayer of Buddha was framed, which won admiration even from a strong opponent among the Brahmans: ' Let all the sins that have been committed in ' this Kali age of the world fall on me, and let the ' world be delivered.'   In this spirit the historian of Ceylon speaks of the devotion of the early Buddhist missionaries there : ' who following the ' example of the all-compassionating vanquisher's ' resignation (of his supreme beatitude), laid aside ' the exalted state of happiness attained by them ' for the benefit of mankind, and undertook these ' missions to various countries.' ' Who is there,' he adds, ' who would demur when the salvation of ' the world (is at stake)' (Turnour, *Mahawanso*, c. xii. p. 75).

The view given here of the self-devotion of Buddha brings out the characteristic Buddhist idea already noticed, that all finite individual existence, however happy, is evil. A man must seek to escape equally from the personal reward for well-doing and from the personal punishment for evil-doing. Both require a new birth, and from this the Buddhist shrinks.

The cause of this shrinking from a fresh material embodiment is obvious. All personal happiness, like personal pain, carries with it the sentence of perishing. Lasting peace must be found elsewhere.

And what then was this goal—Nirvâna, blowing out, extinction—which was to crown the acquisition of perfect knowledge and to be the salvation of the world? Later Buddhist writers have differently interpreted the word, and it is at present differently interpreted in Buddhist communities. Among European scholars the general opinion has been that it conveys the notion of absolute annihilation. Undoubtedly there is sufficient authority for this sense of the word, but it is difficult to believe that Gautama so taught *Nirvâna.* He was a moralist rather than a metaphysician. The foundation of his morality was sacrifice : the end of his morality was the consummation of sacrifice. It was enough for him to teach that man could hope to cast aside all that was finite, and for the rest not to inquire what then remained. That was a mys-

tery which could be left.   It belonged to a realm
on which man could not presume to enter.   According to words attributed to him, 'The ideas of
' being and not being do not admit of discussion.'
All that he was concerned with was the extinction
of finite being, for the finite self in all its forms,
was, as he assumed, an evil.   The fact that
Nirvâna can, according to his teaching, be gained
in life gives to it a positive character, over which,
as it is conceived, the change of death can have
no power.   Human logic is unable to draw nega-
tive deductions from present experience as to the
possibilities of existence.

Similar reflections seem also to hold good
with regard to the charge of speculative Atheism
which has been brought against Buddhism.   The
earliest Buddhist writings neither affirm nor deny
anything as to an Absolute Being.   On this
momentous subject they preserve a deep silence.
It could hardly have been otherwise.   Apart from
the Incarnation it is hopelessly difficult to form
any clear idea of GOD without introducing an-
thropomorphic limitations, which cannot, as we
feel, properly apply to Him.   To the Buddhists all
limitations are of the nature of evil, and so they
shrank from every definite conception of GOD;
but no less all their teaching seems to require

for its foundation and background that which is infinite, eternal, unchangeable, holy.

But while this thought of the Absolute appears to underlie necessarily all Buddhist morality and is supposed still to *be* when every finite being has reached *Nirvána*, yet the fact remains that, as far as the practical conduct of life is concerned, strict Buddhism is without GOD. It leaves no place for worship or for prayer or for a sacrificial priesthood: the believer has no support and no motive outside himself and his fellow-creatures.

But nature is stronger than any one part of nature; and the history of Buddhism shews that worship is as real a necessity for man as knowledge and discipline. The legends represent Buddha as an object of adoration even during his lifetime; and afterwards his relics and his images have been made the centres of actual, if unauthorised, worship. The unbloody offerings of flowers and perfumes before the gigantic solemn images which symbolise unbroken rest bear witness to an instinct which cannot be repressed. Man will pay honour to the noblest that he knows; and if Buddhism affirmed that the perfect man is the limit of the definite form of the divine which can be shaped by human imagination, it only foreshadowed the form in which GOD has been pleased to make Himself known to us.

The actual circumstances of the spread of Buddhism bear witness to this necessity of worship and of hope in a religion for men, which the theory of Buddhism removed from popular apprehension. The Northern Buddhism, which has spread over 'Nepal, Thibet, China, 'Japan, Mongolia,' gives scope to both in the most concrete shapes; and the current views of religious duties and of the unseen world have degenerated into the grossest superstitions.

It is however unnecessary to trace these corruptions and modifications of Buddhism. The true vitality of Buddhism, and therefore its interest for us, lies in the moral principles of love and sacrifice which we have considered.

(iii)   ZOROASTRIANISM.

The religions of India, Hinduism and Buddhism, were based, as we have seen, upon partial interpretations of nature. Hinduism fell under the dominion of forms of thought which belong to the material world from which it sought deliverance. Buddhism started from an intellectual apprehension of man's constitution which essentially excluded worship. The issue towards which Hinduism looked was a re-absorption of the individual in the Absolute Being. In Buddhism no definite place was assigned to an Absolute Being; and the end of the individual, when he was freed from the painful bonds of his limitations, was left as a mystery unfathomable and ineffable. Both systems were obviously incomplete; both refused to deal with problems which continually present themselves. They took no account of the whole man or of his aspirations, as a unity, to a continuous existence.

The third great Aryan religion, Zoroastrianism, was a splendid attempt to deal with the world and man as integral parts of a divine scheme in their totality. Body and soul, the seen and the unseen, evil and good, were set over against one another, and some approach, at least, was made to reconcile them in a provisional synthesis. For the future, a hope of resurrection took the place of absorption or extinction. For the present, sunshine and waters and fields were looked upon as glorious works of a beneficent Creator.

There seems to be no sufficient reason to doubt the historical reality of Zarathustra Spitama (Zerdusht, Zoroaster) the traditional founder of Zoroastrianism; though his date cannot be fixed

with any certainty. It has indeed been argued
that the earliest portions of the Zend-Avesta
offer sufficient grounds for determining the
chronological relation of his teaching to successive forms of Indian religion. The *Devas*, the gods
of Hinduism, are the evil spirits of Zoroastrianism.
The beneficent powers, the *Ahuras* of Zoroastrianism, are the enemies of the gods in the Hindu
mythology. Indra, one of the greatest of the
Vedic gods, is first among the demons who are
reckoned in the train of Angra-Mainyu. From
these facts it has been concluded that Zoroastrianism was the result of a bitter struggle with
Hinduism; and in fact a revolt from Brahminism
shortly after the primitive Vedic faith had been
consolidated into a practical polytheism, and yet
before the ideas of caste and incarnation and
transmigration, and of the Trimurti had become
current.

Such conclusions cannot be pressed with great
confidence. The systems of Zoroastrianism and
Brahminism may have been parallel developments under different circumstances of the same
original elementary belief; for it is clear that
Zoroastrianism found its starting point in the
primitive Vedic faith. The angel Mithra for
example is identical with the Vedic Mitra; and
the prominence of Agni in the Vedic hymns

points to a time when fire was the most common
emblem of divine action even among Indian
worshippers. In fact express mention is made
in the Zend-Avesta of fire-priests (Soshyantos)
earlier than Zarathustra. Thus perhaps for a
time the movements towards the Brahmanic and
the Zoroastrian faith may have existed side by side,
when the heroic genius of Zarathustra brought
their rival claims to a decisive conflict. Or the
two systems may have grown up independently
in separate regions and under the influence of
different local conditions. Yet on the whole there
appears to be a distinct polemical element in the
earliest Zoroastrian Hymns; and the contrast between Zoroastrianism and early Brahminism is no
less political than religious. On the one side were
the settled tillers of the ground: on the other side
adventurous nomads; and the intense hatred of
the Indian *Devas* among the Iranians may have
been partly due to the success which they were
supposed to bring their worshippers in their attacks
upon the homesteads of their neighbours.

Without attempting to define more exactly the
relation of the two divergent types to their common
stock, it may be reasonably supposed that when the
Aryan tribes of Bactria and North India were on
the point of disruption (about 1500—1000 B.C.)

Zarathustra arose to organise his Iranian countrymen and purify their faith. He found powerful
supporters, and yet at times he speaks as one who
knew the bitterness of apparent failure. 'To
'what land to turn; aye, whither turning shall I go ?
'On the part of a kinsman prince or allied peer,
'none, to conciliate, give offerings to me to help my
'cause, nor yet the throngs of labour, not even such
'as these, nor yet, still less, the evil tyrants of the
'province...This I know, Mazda !...Therefore I cry
'to Thee; behold it, Lord! desiring helpful grace
'for me, as friend bestows on friend' (*Yasna* xlvi.
1 f., S. B. E. xxxi. 135 ; comp. *Yasna* xxix. 9). None
the less his work was done; and one of the earliest
Gâthâs describes the scene of his appeal to the
multitudes assembled before him. Even if the
details of the translation are confessedly uncertain,
the general scope of the Hymn is clear, and for a
moment the figure of this earliest and greatest
of Gentile prophets stands out, like Joshua at
Shechem or Elijah on Carmel, as he offers to
the people the choice between the service of
Ahura Mazda and the service of the devas,
between good and evil, by the side of the holy
fire (*Yasna* xxx.).

The message which Zarathustra had to give
was not unworthy of such an introduction. He

had gained views of GOD, of the world, and of man, which approach more nearly to the fulness of truth than anything else which heathen literature can shew. These views he expressed with singular simplicity, and by constant iteration stamped them for all time upon the sacred writings of his successors. There is indeed something almost Shemitic in the stern monotony with which he sets forth his principles, and in the faithfulness with which the Zoroastrians afterwards guarded them from the assaults of polytheism.

The compound title which Zarathustra gave to the Supreme Being, Ahura Mazda, gradually contracted through the forms Ahuramazda, Auramazda, Ahurmazd, Auharmazd into the modern Persian and Parsee Hormazd and Ormazd, marks at once the connexion of his theology with the ancient faith and also its distinctness. His predecessors had worshipped many *Ahuras*, living ones. He concentrated this conception of life upon one *Ahura*, the living one. The second part of the title (Mazda) is of uncertain meaning. It has been interpreted 'the wise' or 'the bestower of intelligence' and also 'the creator of the universe.' Whichever sense be finally established the thought is equally sublime. Whether we take ' the living, the wise' or 'the living, the Creator' as the

Zoroastrian designation of GOD, He is alike brought into a real and direct relation with finite beings.

In this name then, Ahura Mazda, we catch a glimpse of the idea of Zoroastrianism. The names of GOD in any religious system are naturally the best indications of the characteristic doctrine of GOD. For such names are so many declarations of opinions as to His nature, even as we find in the Old Testament that the names of GOD are severally revelations of GOD. And this name Ahura Mazda does not stand alone. Other names to the number of twenty which are enumerated in the Ormazd-Yasht combine to give a lively picture of Zarathustra's Theology. These names are declared as offering the most effectual protection against evil spirits. To utter a particular name of GOD is in fact to confess a particular attribute and to appeal to Him under this aspect of His power. Among the names are the following: 'the One of whom questions are asked' (i.e. the Revealer of truth), 'Perfect Holiness,' 'Understanding,' 'the All-seeing One,' 'the healing One,' 'the Creator' (S. B. E. xxiii. pp. 4 f.).

This Sovereign Being—the Living One—is at once Light and the source of light, Wisdom and the source of wisdom: the father of all truth:

the giver of truth of speech and sincerity of action and health and immortality and wealth and devotion. From Him, as their last cause, all things come, 'the good and the naught mind, in 'thought and word and deed.'[1]

The attempt to give distinctness to this last conception that that which is naught or evil must be referred ultimately to Ahura Mazda, led to the only important modification of Zarathustra's teaching which gained acceptance in later times, by which the philosophical dualism of Zarathustra was transformed into a theological dualism. Zarathustra himself seems to have taught a certain duality in the one Divine Being, so as to admit that He was the source of happiness and sorrow, of good and evil, of day and night, of life and death. This was expressed by supposing that there were two Spirits in Him, a white Spirit (Spenta-mainyu) and a dark Spirit (Angra-mainyu), united as 'twins' in some ineffable way, as the 'two creators.' But while this was so, the dark Spirit included, so to speak, in essence only the potentiality of evil. There was not in this view

[1] *Yasna* xlvii. 1; xlviii. 4, Haug's *Essays*, pp. 156 f. The translation of Mills is very different, but the rendering of Haug, even if untenable, expresses well Zoroastrian ideas which can be gained elsewhere.

any coordinate eternal rival of the good. Actual
evil was to be crushed. GOD Himself had no
coequal adversary[1].

It was almost necessary that such a doctrine
should be popularly corrupted. The white Spirit
was made to represent the whole being of Ahura
Mazda: the dark Spirit was converted into a
separate and independent power, and as Ahriman
was placed at the head of the forces of evil over
against Ormazd in an eternal conflict. At the
same time each of these adverse potentates was
surrounded with a court. The six chief gifts of
Ahura Mazda were personified and as the six
Amesha spentas (Amshashpends), immortal spirits,
were gathered round Him as a council, by the
side of whom was Serosh (Sraosha), the representative of religious service, the great angel who
stands between GOD and man, as mediator and
protector. So too Ahriman had his legates (six
in the later texts), among whom Indra the

---

[1] The earliest expression of dualism (*Yasna* xxx. 3) speaks
of 'two spirits,' two principles, 'a better thing and a worse,'
and not of two persons. It may perhaps be illustrated by
Xen. *Cyrop.* vi. 1, 41. The question is however one of extreme
difficulty; but the supremacy of good seems to be affirmed
equally in the earliest and latest forms of Zoroastrian doctrine,
though opinion fluctuated in the course of its development.

chief of the Vedic gods, occupied the second place.

Thus a final dualism was substituted for the original Zoroastrian monotheism, and from this source dualistic doctrines invaded the Christian Church in Gnosticism and Manichæism. But this dualism is not final in the true system of Zoroastrianism. The powers of evil are at last wholly defeated. Hell itself is made pure by a cleansing fire. 'The renovation arises by the ' will [of Ahura Mazda] and the world is immortal ' for ever and everlasting.'

The Zoroastrian doctrine of the world closely approximates to that of the Bible. Creation is not an illusion or an evil. 'The waters and the ' trees and the luminaries' are of the good work of Ahura Mazda. He made them: to Him they belong: and He is 'the animating spirit of' 'nature.' By His power, working through His legions of guardian angels, all the beneficent processes of life are sustained (*Fârvardîn Yasht* 1 ff.; S. B. E. xxiii. 180 ff.).

And as the revolutions of the world are due to Divine influence so also they are supposed to contribute to the Divine glory. 'The stars, suns, ' and the Aurora which brings on the light of days,

'are all, through their Righteous Order, the
'speakers of Thy praise, O Thou Great Giver,
'Lord' (*Yasna* l. 10; S. B. E. xxxi. 175).

The Zoroastrian doctrine of man is not less
striking than the doctrine of the world. It is
equally removed from the materialistic slavery of
Hinduism and from the absolute self-sacrifice of
Buddhism. It is more personal than cosmical or
social. Man stands forth in his full being and
holds converse with the Divine powers. He is
one in his entire nature and looks forward to
future life answering to the present. He serves
Ahura Mazda 'with body and soul.' Ceremonial
purity is insisted on as complementary to moral
purity but not as a substitute for it. Man has in
fact two lives and two intellects. The one life is
earthly and the other is spiritual : the one intellect is the result of manifold experience, 'the
'wisdom gained by the ear'; the other is an
original Divine gift, 'heavenly wisdom' (Haug,
Essays, p. 264). And the constant specification
of 'thought, word and deed' in the Zend-Avesta
is a characteristic mark of the care with which
Zarathustra inculcated the completeness of religious service.

The importance of words carried with it the

paramount value of Truth in speech.   Hence
Truth and Lies are opposed in the Zend-Avesta as
Light and Darkness, Good and Evil; and it was
by truthfulness that the Persian empire grew
strong.   Truth of thought, right belief, was held
to be no less important than truth of word.   The
first of the five deadly sins was 'to teach one of
'the faithful a foreign Creed' (*Vend.* Fargard xv.
1).   So the whole duty of man is summed up in
a memorable sentence: 'Purity is for man, next
'to life, the greatest good, that purity that is
'procured by the law of Mazda to him who
'cleanses his own self with good thoughts, words,
'and deeds' (*Vend.* Fargard v. 21 ; S. B. E. iv. p. 55).

Equally characteristic of the Zoroastrian idea
of the right type of life is the constant praise of
agriculture.   Man is not born for roving violence,
or for indolent tending of flocks, but for a settled
home and to win from the earth the blessings
which she is waiting to give.   'He who sows
'corn' so spoke Ahura Mazda 'sows holiness: he
'makes the law of Mazda grow higher and higher
'...When wheat is coming forth the Daêvas are
'destroyed'(*Vend.* Fargard iii. 31 f.; S. B. E. iv. 29 f.).

The doctrine of the 'last things' is perhaps
the most important contribution of Zoroastrianism

to the original expression of man's religious
consciousness. Elsewhere a future existence was
connected with the doctrine of transmigration.
Zarathustra fixed the ideas of a Heaven and a
Hell as answering to man's conduct in his time of
trial on earth. Heaven is 'a house of hymns':
Hell is 'a house of destruction.' The passage to
Heaven is by the Bridge of Kinvat over which
the good alone can cross, guided by the angel
Serosh.

In one of the Yashts a picture is drawn of
the fate of souls after death, that recals many
features in the myth at the close of Plato's
Republic which is said to have been of Zoroastrian origin. For three nights the souls wait by
their bodies in the greatest pleasure or pain, and
afterwards they see as it were their own con-
sciences coming towards them in the shape of a
beautiful maiden or a hideous hag, according as
their lives have been, and they are brought in
four steps through the paradises of Good-thought,
Good-word, and Good-deed to the region of Endless
Light, or through the hells of Evil-thought, Evil-
word, and Evil-deed to the region of Endless
Darkness (*Yasht* xxii; S. B. E. xxiii. 314 ff.; comp.
Yasht xxiv. 53 ff.; *Vend.* Fargard xix. 27 ff.; *Bun-
dehesh* xxx).

But the reward of the good was not limited to

the happiness of their souls. In due time their bliss was to be consummated by a resurrection. For this end a great prophet Saoshyant (Soshyos), a supernatural son of Zaráthustra, was to be born, who should awaken and judge the dead and slay death and destroy all the works of devils. Thenceforth the world will never grow old or die ; 'life 'and immortality will come and the world will be 'restored at its wish' (*Zamyâd Yasht* 89 f.; S. B. E. xxiii. 306 f.).

From this rapid sketch it will be evident that Zarathustra is not wholly unworthy to be placed as a Gentile by the side of Abraham. But there is this essential difference between them. Abraham in obedience to the Divine call broke completely with the idolatrous worship of his fathers and threw himself wholly upon the unseen. Zarathustra endeavoured to purify and use the natural emblems to which his countrymen were attached. As a natural result Abraham became the father of the faithful to the end of time, the first in a long line of interpreters of the Divine will. Zarathustra enveloped his message in a service which tended continually to overpower it (comp. *Yasna* xix. 6 ; S. B. E. xxxi. 261), and no successor arose to carry forward in its loftiest form a work which he had already brought down to earth.

CHAPTER VI.

PRESUPPOSITIONS OF THE CHRISTIAN SOLUTION.

ALL religion, as we have seen, assumes the existence of self, the world, and GOD, and deals with the problems to which these three ultimate elements of our knowledge give rise. Christianity, in this following Judaism which was its special preparation, makes three assumptions as to these existences, and claims that the assumptions are justified by the intuitions and experience of men. It assumes, that the world was made by GOD (Gen. i. 1): that man was made in the image of GOD (Gen. i. 27): that man by self-assertion has broken his rightful connexion with GOD (Gen. iii. 9—24). It follows from these assumptions that the world is for the Christian in all its parts an expression of the will of GOD: that man can hold fellowship with GOD: that man needs the help of GOD for the fulfilment of his destiny, in the sense that he requires not only growth but restoration.

These assumptions are found, I believe, to receive the amplest justification in life. They form the adequate basis for a comprehensive and harmonious view of the facts which fall within our knowledge. But they are made subject to all the limitations which belong to us as men. They leave the difficulties which in the last place necessarily beset all human thought unremoved. All our conceptions are defined by conditions of time and space, which belong only to beings such as we are now, and are obviously provisional. We cannot, for example, as has been already noticed, form a clear idea of time or space as either limited or unlimited. We cannot again reconcile in the way of reason the cöexistence of the finite and the infinite. We cannot explain the origin of evil. These ultimate and insoluble difficulties remain. As men on earth we cannot escape from them. They set their mark upon all our thoughts as human thoughts. And under these limitations, these imperfections of vision, our views of things are necessarily shaped.

In Christianity then it is assumed, I repeat,

with a full recognition of these fundamental
and final difficulties, that GOD made and rules
the world in righteousness.   It is assumed that
man can hold personal converse with GOD.   It
is assumed that the completeness of this potential communion between GOD and man has been
marred by sin, the act of man as a responsible
agent, which yet is not irremediable.

These propositions are everywhere taken for
granted in the Bible as expressing truths which
each man is able to recognise as truths when
they are presented to him in an intelligible
form.   They are not explained or justified, but
summarily affirmed or more frequently implied.
They are not presented as elements of a specific
revelation, but they are taken as the basis of all
revelation.   They are put forward, so to speak, as
the Preface to the whole record of Holy Scripture,
which is itself in its fulness the record of the
gradual unfolding of the Divine counsel and work.
They are indeed literally the Preface to the Bible;
for in this respect the opening chapters of Genesis,
which have been most unhappily obscured by a
flood of irrelevant controversy, bring out the
fundamental conditions which make revelation at
once possible and necessary.

We go back therefore to ' *a beginning* ' in our
endeavour to grasp the full import of the Christian

message. From this point of view the whole
narrative of the Creation and the Fall, and not
one isolated verse, contains, when rightly apprehended, the real *Protevangelium*, the primitive
Gospel of the world. That narrative presents in
a vivid form the truths which stand out more or
less distinctly in all the following Books. But it
differs from most other parts of Scripture in this,
that the lessons which it conveys do not lie in the
details of the narrative but in the general ideas
which the narrative embodies.

It would probably be quite impossible for us
(or for man, as he is, at any time) to apprehend
the exact circumstances of Creation, or of the
original constitution of man, or of the Fall. Language must be to the last inadequate to express
the results of perfect observation. But that which
it concerns us to know as to the religious import
of the origin and destiny of finite being is written
in the cardinal sentences which sum up the
contents of our divine Book of Origins.

In the beginning GOD *created the heaven and
the earth...And* GOD *saw every thing that He had
made, and behold it was very good.* Gen. i. 1,
31 *a.*

And GOD *said Let us make man in our image,
after our likeness: and let them have dominion...
So* GOD *created man in His own image, in the*

image of GOD *created He him: male and female created He them.* Gen. i. 26, 27.

And the Lord GOD *called unto Adam and said unto him Where art thou? And he said I heard Thy voice in the garden, and I was afraid, because I was naked; and I hid myself....* Gen. iii. 9, 10, 23, 24.

These passages, which no criticism can rob of their sublime majesty and pathos, form, as I have said, the primitive Gospel of the world, the outline of the Divine promises of love in the essential circumstances of creation and the sequel of creation. They vindicate their prophetic cha-racter as soon as they are placed in comparison with any corresponding ethnic conceptions of the origin and being of the world. The Revelation which they convey is wholly unaffected by the view which may be taken of the incidents which embody the doctrinal statements in a concrete form; and, indeed, a careful examination of the narrative seems to leave no doubt that these first scenes in the religious history of the world are described in a symbolic form, even as the last scenes portrayed in the Apocalypse. For both —for the beginning and the end—this form, as we may reasonably believe, is, from the neces-sity of the case, that which is best suited to

convey to a being like man the right impression
of the truths shadowed out.

What then are the truths which they convey?
We return to the fundamental passages in our
'Book of Origins.'

In the beginning GOD *created the heaven and
the earth...And* GOD *saw every thing that He had
made, and behold it was very good.*   Gen. i. 1,
31 a.

The first thing which strikes the student in
the opening verse of the Bible is that GOD is at
once represented as acting.   Neither here nor
elsewhere is the simple fact of His existence
asserted, nor are His abstract attributes set forth.
It is assumed that men have the idea of GOD, and
then His Character is portrayed in His ·works.
To deny His existence is the mark of the fool
(Ps. xiv. 1).   Forgetfulness of GOD is the guilt
of the heathen (Ps. ix. 17 [18]).   The nations
who were without GOD had been estranged from
Him to Whom they properly belonged (Eph.
ii. 12).   GOD is represented as making Himself
known in answer to the instinctive language of
the heart which found expression in idolatry.
'*I even I am He*' (ἐγώ εἰμι LXX.)—He Whom
man looks for in the unseen world—'*and there is
no* GOD *with me*' (Deut. xxxii. 39).   '*I am He*'...

' *I even I am the Lord, and beside me there is no
Saviour.*' ' *Yea before the day was I am He* '
(Is. xliii. 10, 11, 13). '*Even to your old age I am
He*' (Is. xlvi. 4). ' *I am the first I also am the
last* ' (Is. xlviii. 12; comp. Is. xli. 4, and Delitzsch
or Cheyne; Ps. cii. 27). And so the believer
answers ' *Thou art* GOD *alone*' (Is. xxxvii. 16).
Thus the whole teaching of Scripture is directed
to shew not that GOD is, nor yet what He is in
Himself, but what He is in His dealings with
men; or in other words to make Him known in
various ways through the historical manifestations
of His holiness and His love. From first to last
this is the one message of prophets and apostles,
in many parts and in many fashions, in judgments
and in warnings, that message which found a clear
enunciation in ' the last time ': GOD *is love* (1 John
iv. 8, 16), as crowning the other declarations:
GOD *is spirit* (John iv. 24) and GOD *is light*
(1 John i. 5), and *our* GOD *is a consuming fire*
(Hebr. xii. 29; Deut. iv. 24).

In this light the Biblical statement as to
Creation is seen in its true relation to all that
follows. Two principles which underlie all religious conceptions of the world are plainly affirmed
in it. The creation and disposition of the whole
order in which we live was the work of GOD, and,

as we are able to apprehend it, the work of creation was regulated and completed in accordance with a definite plan. Or to express the truths otherwise, the whole finite order was due only to the will of GOD, and it answered to that will perfectly. These points it concerns us to know; and they obviously do not fall within the province of human observation. On the other hand when these truths are laid down, it remains for us to investigate, as we can, how they are realised, so far as they fall under our notice. In one sense it is said '*GOD rested on the seventh day from all His work which He had made*' (Gen. ii. 2), and in another sense it is said '*My Father worketh hitherto and I work*' (John v. 17). Relatively to GOD we must regard 'all creation' as 'one act at once'; but relatively to ourselves we necessarily break up the one creative act into many parts that so we may realise it better. In this relation it would not be difficult to point out the fitness and symmetry of the distribution of the parts of the Divine work through the six days from the point of sight assumed by the writer of Genesis. He looks at things from the earth as centre, and regards them in due succession according to obvious sensible characteristics. From another point of sight the same thought of order might offer itself under another form. Such considerations have also a wider application. According to our powers or knowledge we may present GOD to ourselves as working in this way or that, uniformly, so to speak, or interruptedly. And these different modes of conception are not without moral significance, but they are only of secondary importance : that which is essential is that we should keep firm hold of the one immutable truth that GOD made all that is, and that all, as He made it, was very good.

The second passage brings out another thought. The creation was consummated in man, '*the image and glory of GOD*' (1 Cor. xi. 7).

And GOD said Let us make man in our image, after our likeness : and let them have dominion... So GOD created man in His own image, in the image of GOD created He him : male and female created He them. Gen. i. 26, 27.

One thing at least is clear from these words that, according to the teaching of Scripture, man stands in a position of exceptional nearness to GOD ; and the corresponding words in the second chapter confirm the truth under a different aspect (ii. 7). There is, to express the thought otherwise, such a relation between man and GOD, that man is fitted by his essential constitution to receive a knowledge of GOD. Revelation is made possible

for him from the first. He is not confined to
thoughts which are suggested to him by self-
examination or by the study of creation: he is
capable of apprehending divine truths, he can
learn concerning GOD what GOD is pleased to
teach, without any essential change in his original
constitution. The conception of GOD'S Nature
and mode of working may be above his imagination, but it is not above his power of apprehension.

This unique position of man in the visible
order is emphasised by other details. He has
dominion over other creatures (i. 28): he assigns
to them their names (ii. 19 f.): he finds among
them no companion fitted for himself (ii. 18, 20).
As he appears first in his true nature he is 'little
lower than a divine being' (Ps. viii.), at perfect
peace in himself, towards nature, and towards
GOD. He is made for GOD and, to this end, he is
made 'in the image of GOD.'

It is difficult indeed to define exactly in what
sense man was made 'in the image of GOD.'
Perhaps we can do no more than hold that in his
whole being he is, in his true nature, fitted to
represent GOD to us in the present order (comp.
Ezek. i. 26). This thought appears to be suggested by the Incarnation (Col. i. 15), whereby
the glory of man (Ps. viii. 6) is fully realised

(Hebr. ii. 6 ff.). There is at least no authority
for separating any one part of man as alone
presenting the image. Holiness, which we feel
to be the most god-like quality in man, involves
the cooperation and consecration of all his powers
and endowments.

In this relation it is important to notice
that we are concerned with man as man, as
endowed with this faculty of Divine communion.
It is of no moment for us to inquire in this place
through what stages (if any) he reached this
point, any more than it is to inquire in this
respect into the stages through which the individual passes before his natural birth. The theory
of development has no religious significance
here. Development is only a way of writing
out the Divine method of working according to
the form of human apprehension.

And further: while man as man was made
with a capacity for receiving knowledge of GOD,
the knowledge was not directly given in its
fulness. In this respect the contrast between the
account of the Divine purpose and of the Divine
work is most significant. *GOD said, Let us make
man in our image, after our likeness...So GOD
created man in His own image.* Man was not
created in his ideal completeness, but such that he

was in a position to attain to it by freely using the Divine help which was offered to him. He was not, as GOD's good work, finally perfect, but only potentially perfect. He was created in the image of GOD, and he had to gain progressively by cooperation with GOD the likeness of GOD for which he was made. The constitution, the powers, are given: the character is wrought out in life. Such a view brings to its ultimate antithesis and ultimate harmony finite freedom and an infinite and loving will. It reconciles the claims of human morality and of Divine grace in their last form. Man in and by himself is neither perfect nor capable of attaining perfection; but he was made capable of attaining perfection by using the gifts placed within his reach and by working with GOD.

This brings us to the third point in the Divine portraiture of man's religious position. He failed through self-will to fulfil his right destiny.

And the Lord GOD called unto Adam, and said unto him, Where art thou? And he said, I heard Thy voice in the garden, and I was afraid, because I was naked; and I hid myself... Gen. iii. 9, 10, 23, 24.

The absolute, childlike, freedom of the communion between GOD and man is here seen to

have been interrupted. The picture answers to
universal experience. There is something in us
to be hidden: something of which we are ourselves ashamed. So far we are only placed face
to face with an unquestionable fact. But Revelation illuminates the fact which it recognises.
This interruption is shewn to be due to the
action of some power distinct from ourselves.
It does not belong to the essence of our nature,
and therefore it can be remedied. The very Fall
in its consummation is so brought about that it
leaves man still man, and therefore still retaining
essentially GOD'S image.

This truth finds distinct expression at the
second religious starting-point of the human race.
In the Covenant with Noah the life of man is
declared to be sacred '*for in the image of GOD
made He man*' (Gen. ix. 6), where the argument
requires that the image should still remain, and
not merely once have been. And so St Paul
speaks of man as man being 'the image (εἰκών)
and glory of GOD' (1 Cor. xi. 7); though being
what he is he needs continuous renewal to gain
his ideal state (Col. iii. 10; comp. James iii. 9;
Luke xv. 8).

The sense of this fact, illuminated by the
promise connected with the Fall, explains the

remarkable silence throughout the Old Testament
as to the Fall itself. The Jew did not dwell with
a regretful retrospect on a lost Paradise: his
thoughts were turned to a more glorious future.

While therefore we must keep firm hold on
the fact of the Fall and on the consequences of
the Fall, we must not exaggerate the change
which it brought to man. The 'original righteousness' which he lost can best be conceived of
as the result of the harmonious development of
life under the action of the Divine Communion.
In one sense this was natural, so far as it answered
to the Divine purpose for man: in another sense
it was supernatural, so far as the power by which
it was wrought was not in man but from GOD.
When the fellowship was broken the continuous
support necessary for perfect and progressive
holiness was withdrawn. Yet conscience bears
witness to the destiny for which man was made
and which by himself he cannot reach.

It does not fall within the scope of our
present subject to pursue the interpretation of
these passages at greater length. It must be
enough to point out again that our 'Book of
Origins' furnishes the unchanging basis of our
religious belief, that it sets before us in a shape
most simple and most pregnant a Divine inter-

pretation of the facts of which we are conscious; and yet further that the record of the Creation and of the Fall is first apprehended in its full significance when it is studied as a revelation of spiritual mysteries and not as a realistic narrative : that nothing is lost in the value of the details when they are regarded as symbolical and not as historical: that in fact the details do not grow luminous till they are interpreted as the expression of thoughts thus brought vividly before the imagination. The lessons which are given by this Preface to all Revelation, are in short moral and spiritual, and not physical and historical. They lay down irrevocably the essential relations of GOD, and man, and the world. They go back to a point beyond all experience. The final sanctions of every noble form of human activity, the promises which illuminate " the toppling crags of duty," are implicitly contained in them. They shew that the order of finite being corresponds with a counsel of GOD and has been called out, as it falls under our observation, in an orderly sequence. They shew that the blessing with which it was crowned, if hindered, has not been revoked. They shew that the conception of humanity as a living whole is not a dream but a truth. They shew that the aspirations of man to GOD answer to his essential constitution and contain the pledge

of fulfilment. They shew that the sinfulness by
which he is bound and the sins by which he is
stained are not parts of his real self: that they
are intrusive and that so they can be done away.
Thus the great facts of our earthly existence are
from the first placed in connexion with an
unseen order; and then in due course throughout
the Bible the later phases of this connexion are
traced out in their critical succession. We are, as
has been said before, not concerned with the
'how' but with the 'that,' of the Creation and
the Fall, not with the manner but with the fact.
It may be that whole cycles of existence are
summarised in the words '*God created man in
His own image*' (Gen. i. 27); and '*the Lord
God formed man of the dust of the ground, and
breathed into his nostrils the breath of life*' and
'*man became a living soul*' (Gen. ii. 7). It may
be that whole cycles of progressive probation,
manifold issues of preparatory experience, are
gathered up in the Fall. But the great facts
remain in their momentous significance, though
they are clothed for us in a mystical dress.

For the most part the facts of the Creation
and the Fall are apprehended individually through
feeling and experience. This individual witness
is enough for the guidance of life. And it cannot
be without a profound meaning that the record of

the Fall is not noticed once unquestionably in the
later books of the O. T., and only twice in the
Apocrypha, till the fact of the Incarnation had
enabled men to understand its import.

Its teaching was, so to speak, latent; but
while the details of the records of the Creation
and of the Fall are but rarely referred to in
the Bible, the facts and the doctrines—that is
the interpretations of the facts—which they
preserve, the three postulates of religion, are
universally affirmed.

In this respect it will be sufficient to notice
the language of St Paul.   In the book of the Acts
brief summaries are given of words which he
addressed on two occasions to heathen audiences.
On the first occasion he was pleading against the
misinterpretation of a work of healing, which led
the rude inhabitants of Lystra to offer to him and
Barnabas divine honours (Acts xiv. 15–17).   On
the second occasion he was rendering an account
to educated Athenians of the strange doctrine
which he was alleged to teach (xvii. 22–31).   The
circumstances under which he spoke could hardly
have been more different.   But in both cases his
language as to GOD is essentially the same.   'The
'nations had failed to recognise the Creator and
'Ruler of the world, though He had set about

'them signs of His working. The time of this
'ignorance was now past. A clear message laid
'open the neglected truth ; and (so it is assumed)
'those who heard would find in it the answer to
'their own vague thoughts.' At Athens the Apostle naturally carried on his explanation further,
and laid down distinctly the main propositions
which we have found in the first chapters of the
Bible, the orderly progress of the Divine working
(ὁρίσας προστεταγμένους [προτετ.] καιροὺς καὶ
τὰς ὁροθεσίας τῆς κατοικίας), the Divine image in
man (τοῦ γὰρ καὶ γένος ἐσμέν), the unity of the
human race (ἐποίησε ἐξ ἑνὸς πᾶν ἔθνος ἀνθρώπων),
the universal necessity of repentance (παραγγέλ-
λει τοῖς ἀνθρώποις πάντας πανταχοῦ μετανοεῖν).
These propositions are taken as the foundation of
his appeal : they are assumed to be supported by
'testimonies of the soul naturally Christian.'

In the Epistle to the Romans the same truths
are put forth more formally. Men had, it is
affirmed, a knowledge of GOD as GOD, a knowledge of His eternal power and divinity, from the
time of creation, given openly in His works. They
lacked in this respect not knowledge, but the will
to apply their knowledge : 'Having known GOD,
'they did not glorify Him as GOD ;' and from this
primal wilful sin flowed the full stream of their
degradation (Rom. i. 19-21). Nor was this all :

corresponding with the revelation of GOD without, there was also for man a revelation of GOD within. As the world was His workmanship; so man was made in His image. Up to a certain point therefore He could be discerned in the soul as well as in nature. So in fact men as they knew GOD, knew His sentence on particular modes of action, and set it at naught (Rom. i. 32), or else imperfectly conformed to the law which it indicated (ii. 14, f.).

It would be easy to multiply passages from the Old and New Testaments in which the same assumptions are made; but no attentive student will doubt that the three great postulates as to GOD, the world, and man, which have been specified, form the groundwork of the Biblical history and teaching. It is assumed that they are acknowledged by every one individually as witnessed to by his conscience; and that generally they correspond with what we know of ourselves and of our position in the world. At the same time it is allowed that they have been and can be plausibly denied. No thoughtful man will presume to say that the explanation of the universe which they represent is free from difficulties. Other explanations of our present state may be offered, as in fact they have been offered; or some may refuse to consider any explanation at

202 *The postulates* [CHAP.

all. In such a case it does not appear that there is any certain way of establishing the truths assumed. The utmost that can be done is to shew that any other explanation of the universe is beset by far greater difficulties than that in which they are involved; and that we are impelled by our nature to seek for some explanation of it, and (as we have seen) that the explanation which we adopt must powerfully affect our character.

The Christian postulates cannot be established by independent reasoning, but they can be illustrated by it; and there may be occasions when it is desirable to dwell on such illustrations as can be derived from nature and history: from the constitution of our own minds or from the order and progress of the outer world: from the broad stream of events and the analysis of separate lives; but care must be taken not to overrate their cogency, or to extend their application beyond their proper scope. The idea of GOD (for example) must be admitted before such illustrations are really effective. Nor is there anything exceptionally disadvantageous to religious truth in the necessity for this fundamental assumption. It is just so in daily life. I assume that the men among whom I move are personal beings es-

sentially like myself, and then all experience
contributes to the completeness of my knowledge
of their character. But there is no method of
argument by which I can be overcome if I maintain that other men are creations of my own brain
or irresponsible automata.

And here it will be well to notice a misconcep-
tion which appears to prevail almost universally. It is very commonly asserted by thinkers
of different schools, that GOD is unknowable by
men, and it appears to be implied at the same
time, even when it is not so said, that He is
unknowable in some peculiar sense. But surely
it is true that in themselves men and the world
are as truly unknowable as GOD. All our knowledge of man and of the world and of GOD is
relative and modified by the laws of our own
personal constitution. All our knowledge in other
words is human knowledge into which our human
nature, the conditions of our human senses and
reason, must enter as one factor. It is utterly
impossible for us ever to separate the thought
from the thinking person, to separate what belongs
to man from that unknown something which when
apprehended by him produces such and such an
impression, or is realised in such and such a form.
And this inexorable union of man himself with all
his knowledge does not make his knowledge illu-

sory or evanescent. True (if imperfect) knowledge expresses a right conception (so far as it goes) of the relation of two things, of ourselves and something else. Fuller knowledge will therefore take up and embody partial knowledge. It is so with our knowledge of the constitution of our own minds, and of the outer world, and it is so also with our knowledge of GOD. If, as we assume, man is made to know GOD, through an appropriate organ, as he is made to know himself and the universe through mind and sense, his knowledge of GOD will be like in kind to his knowledge of himself and of the world. GOD, in short, is unknowable and known just as the world is unknowable and known.   •

However, not to pursue such speculations, it is evident that the enunciation of the three postulates of the existence of a righteous Creator and Governor of the world, of the creation of man in the image of GOD, and of the reality of sin, places Christianity in a definite position with regard to some popular difficulties concerning revelation, and this position cannot be too distinctly recognised and made known. For if there is a righteous Creator and Governor of the world it follows that all antecedent objections to 'miracles,' all objections to 'miracles' as distinguished from objections to the evidence alleged in favour of particular miracles, are beside the mark. And again, if man has been created in the image of GOD, the objections against revelation in particular which are based on man's incapacity to rise above himself are met by the particular theory of man's nature which is laid down. And thirdly, if man has fallen from GOD by his responsible ('free') act, the consequent relation of man to GOD is such that he cannot be restored to his original state of perfect communion otherwise than by the action of Divine Love.

CHAPTER VII.

THE assertion which has been made that miracles, 'signs' (σημεῖα), are more properly in their highest form the substance than the proofs of revelation requires to be justified a little more at length. And it must be noticed at the outset that when we speak of any phenomenon as 'miraculous,' we are offering one particular interpretation of it, where many other interpretations are conceivable. It does not follow at once that a phenomenon which is, as far as our experience goes, absolutely unique and wholly unaccountable, even if we have taken pains to become acquainted with all the circumstances connected with it, will be pronounced to be a miracle. And on the other hand it is not difficult to imagine a coincidence of circumstances, all in themselves perfectly intelligible, and as a whole not unexampled, which we should without hesitation call a miracle. On the one hand we are so deeply conscious of the imperfection of our knowledge of the nature and action of forces without and within ourselves, that we may in a particular case find it easier to suppose that we have overlooked some factor in the result or that we have been deceived, than to suppose that we are in the presence of a power manifesting itself personally. And on the other hand there are subtle signs, answering to the experience of common life, which are calculated to force upon us the conviction that in a particular combination of phenomena we are brought face to face with One working directly before us in a way analogous to that in which we work, so far as the fact falls within the range of our observation. These considerations shew that the definitions of a miracle which turn upon particular theories as to causation cannot be maintained. The best idea which we can form of a miracle is that of an event or phenomenon which is fitted to suggest to us the action of a personal spiritual power; and this fitness may lie either in the nature of the phenomenon itself, or in the circumstances of the phenomenon, or in the nature and circumstances of the phenomenon conjointly. A miracle, in other words, is what it is characteristically called in the New Testament, a 'sign' (σημεῖον). Its essence

lies not so much in what it is in itself as in what
it is calculated to indicate.

The phenomenon, I say, which is apprehended as a miracle suggests the idea of the
action of a personal spiritual power. But in
itself it can do no more than suggest the idea of
his action. It is wholly unable in any intelligible
sense to prove the existence of such a power; and
still less to prove that the power is Infinite. It
cannot prove the *existence* of the power, because
experience shews us that the forces which act
about us often lead to results which we could not
have anticipated, and that we cannot presume to
think that there may not be other forces capable
of acting about us which we have not yet detected.
The phenomenon in question may, then, be due to
hitherto unknown combinations of known forces,
or to a force hitherto unknown. It need not be
attributed to a personal spiritual power, though
the action of such a power may be the simplest
and, so far, the most probable explanation of the
phenomenon. And, again, no phenomenon can
prove the existence of an infinite power. Every
manifestation of power which can be made to
us necessarily falls short of that which we can
imagine. The utmost that any particular effect
can require of the observer is that he shall admit

the existence of a power sufficient to produce it.
It cannot in itself justify him in affirming as a
logical conclusion the existence of an agent
endowed with indefinitely greater strength or
wisdom than is adequate to produce the effect for
which he has to account. In other words, the
idea of GOD, in the fulness of His Infinite
attributes, must come from ourselves. It cannot
be established, however distinctly it may be
suggested to us, being what we are, however
plainly it may be illustrated, by that which we
observe without us. Nothing finite can establish
an infinite : no induction in one order can establish
a conclusion in another order.

It must, then, be distinctly admitted that
the very conception of a miracle assumes the
existence of the spiritual power to whose action
the miraculous phenomenon is referred, and whose
character it more fully reveals. In other words,
the possible action of such a Being is added to
the sum of the causes to which we feel ourselves
able to have recourse in the explanation of any
fact which falls under our notice. On such an
assumption there can be no question as to the
possibility of miracles. In each case we shall have
to ask what explanation of the particular fact is
on the whole most reasonable. Is it to be referred

to the regular action of known forces? Or is it to be referred to the action of known forces acting in some way as yet insufficiently determined? Or is it to be referred to the action of some physical force which has hitherto escaped notice? Or is it to be referred directly to the personal action of a spiritual Being? And, further, all these explanations are themselves equally 'natural,' though they may be severally more or less likely. It is quite conceivable that the same phenomenon may under different circumstances admit of different explanations, that a phenomenon which would be recognised as a sign in a particular age or in particular circumstances, would not be recognised as a sign under other conditions. But that on which I wish to insist at present is that the idea of the spiritual Being must precede the idea of the miracle which is referred to His agency, and must be admitted as true before the phenomenon is recognised as a miracle.

This conclusion carries with it important consequences. There will, it follows, be a moral correspondence between the miracles and the Being to whose action they are assigned. So far we have considered generally the case of phenomena which suggest the action of *some* Spiritual power. But it is easy to imagine miracles which would only establish the action of an *evil* power. The assumed character of the spiritual being will therefore determine the assignment of any particular fact to his agency. And here, again, it will be observed that the general conception of the character of the agent must precede the interpretation of the fact: I say the general conception of his character, because the fact may give us further information as to his character, harmonious with our antecedent conception, though not explicitly included in it. Or to express this truth in a different form, the moral bearing of the fact under examination will be a necessary element in our apprehension of it as a miracle, as a Divine sign.

It may, perhaps, appear that these two cardinal propositions, (1) that the idea of a miracle assumes the existence of the spiritual being to whom it is referred, and (2) that our antecedent conception of the character of the being will decide the assignment of any particular fact to his agency, are at variance with popular forms of argument at present, as they are certainly at variance with popular forms of argument in the last century. But whether this be so or not, the propositions are most distinctly assumed in Scripture; and here as elsewhere we must acknow-

ledge with devout gratitude that the thoughts of
the Bible are far deeper than our thoughts, and
survive in their enduring majesty the changing
phases of our modes of speculation. A few passages taken from representative books will place
this assertion beyond contradiction.

In a familiar passage of the book of Deuteronomy (c. xiii) three typical forms of temptation to
apostasy are dealt with, the teaching of a prophet,
who confirms his message by 'a sign or a wonder'
which 'comes to pass' (*vv.* 1 ff.), the persuasion of
kindred (6 ff.), the voice of popular leaders (12 ff.).
In each case the final appeal is to national
and personal experience. Nothing could justly
disturb the trust and love which were thus
established; no miracle, no natural affection, no
hopes of civil prosperity. The trial through the
false prophet, who points to a fulfilment of his
words which is elsewhere made the criterion of
the Divine origin of the sign (xviii. 22), is placed
first and dealt with in fullest detail as the most
crucial of all tests. No question is raised as to
the reality of the phenomenon, or as to its
supernatural character. It is assumed to be
miraculous. But there is a faith in GOD, gained
in life and capable of immediate attestation
through personal devotion, which must be un-

assailable for the believer. Like Abraham he
will trust GOD against sight. No miracle is valid
against a conviction which 'the heart and the
soul' have acknowledged.

In the passage of Deuteronomy the 'sign' by
which GOD tests the love of His people is from
without. The prophet who offers it seeks his
own end in conscious antagonism to the LORD who
uses him for His own purpose. There is a still
more tragical case where the prophet is himself
deceived that he should 'believe the lie' (Ezek.
xiv. 4 ff., 9; comp. 2 Thess. ii. 11), and confirm
in his apostasy the man who seeks counsel from
him when he has himself deliberately chosen his
part and set up idols in his heart. The inquirer
and the answerer have alike cast away the
simplicity of truth, and GOD strengthens their
delusion not as sanctioning it but as making it
the just instrument of their chastisement. There
is that within men which may and ought to
prevail against every outward sign and every
inward voice which the soul has once been able
to recognise as inconsistent with a believer's love.
So temptation is discovered and overcome (comp.
1 K. xxii. 22).

The sovereign responsibility of man is affirmed

with equal clearness in the Gospels. He may
not under any constraint be disloyal to himself.
The Lord lays the duty of personal decision upon
His disciples under circumstances of the sorest
trial. False Christs and false prophets would
arise, when His mission had seemed to close in
failure, and ' shew great signs and wonders, so as
to lead astray, if possible, the elect ' (Matt. xxiv.
23 f.), but having once known Him, that knowledge must be their safeguard. Here again no
question is raised as to the reality of the signs.
Their effect is unquestioned (*vv.* 5, 11). No
promise is given of greater signs. On the contrary
there are sad warnings of peril and loneliness.
But the strength of a personal relationship once
realised is assumed to have adequate source of
strength. Everything that tempts to unfaithful-
ness is met by the assurance : *In your patience ye
shall win your souls* (Luke xxi. 19).

St Paul, in a passage to which reference has
been made already (2 Thess. ii. 8 ff.), combines the
different forms of temptation which simple love
may be called upon to meet and overcome. He
foresees a presence of the lawless one ' according
to the working of Satan with all power and signs
and lying wonders.' The lie which this enemy
shall proclaim shall find credence. The signs

shall lead away some to destruction. And the
apostle lays open the secret of the fall of those
who were deceived: 'they received not the love of
the truth;' they 'had pleasure in unrighteousness.' It was in their power once to welcome
what GOD offered, but they refused the gift, and
so they became the victims of the teacher who
flattered their desires (comp. Gal. i. 8).

One other passage must be quoted in which
St John describes in figures the decisive conflict
of the faith (Apoc. xiii. 11 ff.). The representative of evil 'doeth great signs.' He shews to men
the sign of Elijah, and makes fire to descend out
of heaven (contrast Matt. xvi. 1). The signs are
real, so far as men can test them; and the saints
must meet them only by patience and faith
(Apoc. xiii. 10; xiv. 12). But one significant
phrase reveals the nature of this stern discipline:
'The signs were given to the beast to do.' The
temptation of the disciple corresponds to the
temptation of the Lord (comp. Lk. iv. 6). That
which is most strange and perplexing rests on
the will of GOD. Trust in Him is guidance and
safety.

One great thought, it will be seen, runs
through all these passages, that absolute loyalty

to GOD as recognised and known in the individual
conscience must prevail over every external sign,
and decide on the interpretation of events which
claim to be referred to His action.   Nothing which
is at variance with perfect holiness, and justice,
and truth, can be from Him as a declaration of
His will for us ; and no array of external ' miracles '
can justify us in referring to Him, as authoritative for our direction, any act or word which our
constitution made in His image forces us to regard
as immoral.   And here we must observe that the
distinctness of moral conceptions will correspond
with the growth of the race, as it does with the
growth of the individual, but the essential character of the conceptions will be relatively the same.
Cases may arise in which it is our duty to hold our
judgment in suspense.   We may not be able to
decide as to the real character of a particular act,
and while this is so we must wait in patience for
fuller light ; but nothing can justify us in sacri-
ficing truth or right, felt to be such, to any
alleged works of Him whom we know before all
things to be Light and Love.

It follows from what has been said that the
Bible and reason, the voices of GOD without us
and within us, lead us to believe that GOD, if
He acts, will act according to His Nature, even

as man acts according to his nature, so far, that is, as these acts of GOD fall within the observation of our powers. And this consideration enables us to meet an objection against miracles which ought not to be overlooked. It is urged that when appeal is made to man's power of modifying the course of nature as justifying the belief that GOD also may modify it by 'personal' action, the parallel is unreal. Man, it is urged, uses forces which we see to be adequate to produce the effects attributed to him; and therefore his action offers no real analogy to the alleged action of GOD. But it is obvious that the point of comparison lies not in the mode by which the result is produced, but in the will which (as we are forced to think and speak) is the ultimate spring of action in the two cases. Man acts according to his powers which are regulative; and GOD acts by His energy which is creative. If the alleged Divine action did not suggest the manifestation of creative power it would fail in its characteristic effect. The phenomenon could only suggest an unseen agent like man.

And here it will be well to notice an ambiguity in the word 'omnipotent' as applied to GOD, which appears to have caused strange perplexity to many thoughtful minds. It has been

supposed that omnipotence involves the power of
doing everything. The error is exactly parallel
with that by which freedom in a rational being is
supposed to be compatible with caprice. Freedom
of a rational being can be nothing else than the
power of fulfilling the law of his nature, which is,
under one aspect, complete obedience ; and omnipotence is simply the power of fulfilling the
absolute law of perfection as it is realised. Omnipotence is predicated of Him Who is absolutely
good and holy and righteous, and must be interpreted consistently with these attributes. It
would be a direct contradiction to say that GOD as
omnipotent could do wrong in a particular case, or
make wrong to be right, or cause a thing to be
and not to be at the same time, or that which
has been not to have been, speaking, as we must
speak, according to our limited view. And further,
if it has been the will of GOD (as we assume)
to create a limited free being, this act carries with
it all the consequences involved in any way in the
exercise of that limited freedom, and so far,
according to man's view, necessarily defines the
action of the Divine omnipotence, that is, makes
known the Divine will which is the measure of
the Divine power. The apprehension of this truth,
I may remark, throws light upon the final mystery
of religion, the existence of evil or, more specific-

ally, of sin. Sin in its ultimate form is selfishness
the setting up of itself by the finite against the
Infinite. And the possibility of this is of necessity
included in the idea of a finite self. Self carries
with it the potentiality of isolation. In that
isolation when it becomes a fact there is the
fertilised germ of sin.

To sum up briefly.
It has been shewn that

(1)   A miracle assumes the existence of GOD.

· (2)   That no miracle can justify a man in
referring to GOD that which is immoral as authoritative for man's conduct.

(3)   That miracles, as acts of GOD, will be
essentially creative acts.

(4)   That all the acts of GOD, as omnipotent,
will be (according to our observation) in accordance
with the moral laws which He has made known.

These general considerations on the nature
and character of miracles enable us to apprehend
justly the office which miracles, as historical facts,
and the record of miracles, are fitted to fulfil in
the religious history of man from the Christian
point of view. The case appears to admit of

being stated very plainly. Revelation, which includes the idea of miracles, corresponds with creation. If, as we assume, GOD made the world, and if He made man in His own image, it appears to follow of necessity that He should make Himself known more and more completely, and that, not only in conscience and in nature, but also in life. If man were absolutely isolated, communing with GOD only, then the revelation through conscience would meet the conditions of his existence. If knowledge according to his present powers were the end of his being, then the revelation through the fixed order of the universe would satisfy his wants. But if he is called upon to live, to contend with adverse forces and to conquer, to reach forward to an unseen universe, to realise the eternal through the temporal, then revelation must (to use our human modes of speech) lay open to him something of the Nature of GOD, as disciplining, guiding, sustaining humanity and men. And if further, as is also assumed, man has by his own act interrupted the original communion which he had with GOD and disordered the harmony of his constitution, this likelihood still remains, for GOD still governs the world, and the image of GOD in man if dulled has not been destroyed; and it becomes yet more probable than before that the Divine communications will

take place in (what appear to us) exceptional
ways, and not, so to speak, in the natural and
orderly development of being.

Under these circumstances miracles, as we
have defined the term, are 'natural' vehicles of
revelation; and the records of miracles stand on
the same footing as the records of any other events
connected with the revelation. Internal evidence,
à priori considerations, will come into play here
just as elsewhere, neither more nor less. For
miracles themselves are likely or not according to
the circumstances under which they are stated to
have occurred. They are not isolated, fragmentary
facts, but parts of (what we must regard as being)
a great scheme.

Two practical rules are involved in this view,
and they appear to be essential to the understanding both of the Gospels and of the Gospel.
Every record of a miracle must be considered in
relation, (1) to the whole course of the revelation
of which the miracle is affirmed to be a part, and
(2) to the particular position which the miracle
occupies in that course. No judgment can be
fairly pronounced upon the reality of the miracle
till the historical and moral circumstances by
which it is surrounded are fully grasped.

According to this view it is wrong to speak
of miracles as being in a primary sense proofs
of a revelation, or of Christianity in particular.
No such claim is made for them in the New
Testament. On the contrary, the external testimony of facts is distinctly subordinated to
the testimony of words, that is, to the power
which man is still assumed to possess of recognising the Divine (John xiv. 11 ; xv. 22 ff.; compare also John v. 33 ff.).

A certain condition of faith is required in
those for whom, both in the wider and in the
narrower sense, miracles are wrought (Mk. vi. 5 ;
ix. 23 ; Matt. ix. 28 f.). They are properly a
manifestation of Christ's 'glory,' and those who
can see this are confirmed by them (John ii. 11 ;
xi. 40).

But on the other hand, when the challenge
was given to Christ to shew ' a sign from heaven,'
it was peremptorily declined (Mk. viii. 11 ff.;
Matt. xii. 38 f.; xvi. 1 : notice the use of μοι-
χαλίς).

Miracles are indeed ' signs ' which those who
desire to learn can interpret; but when Christ
Himself refers to the signs which are to supply
the revelation of His character, the last is not the
raising of the dead, but the preaching of a Gospel

to the poor (Matt. xi. 5), in which there is the foreshadowing of the 'greater works' which the disciples were to accomplish (John xiv. 12).

The same law is observable throughout the record of the Apostolic teaching. Miracles were wrought, by the Apostles, so to speak, naturally. They were the flashings forth of the more glorious Divine life when an opening was made for its course. They were not offered as proofs to the unbelieving, but as blessings, and lessons, to the believing. They could be questioned, misinterpreted, denied: they could be accepted as real, and yet carry no conviction of faith (Acts iv. 10, 16 f., 22; xiv. 11, 19).

On the other hand they undoubtedly moved sympathetic witnesses and hearers (iv. 30; viii. 6 ff.; ix. 42; xiii. 12), though the effect was in some cases transient (xiv. 11, 19); and St Peter, speaking both to Jews and Gentiles, appeals to Christ's works of power and love as witnessing to the presence of GOD with Him (ii. 22; x. 38).

The treatment of the Resurrection—the sovereign sign, the sovereign revelation—in the narrative of the Acts illustrates the Apostolic view of miracles. The fact of the Resurrection is treated as the key to a great mystery, the suffer-

ings of the Christ (Acts ii. 24, 31). Appeal is
made to the gift of the Spirit as the sign of the
Resurrection, rather than to the Resurrection as
the proof of the message (v. 32). The Resurrection
itself was the message, not as being an overwhelming wonder, but so far as it was recognised as the
beginning of a new life (xiii. 33). By raising
Christ from the dead GOD 'gave assurance to all
men' of a coming judgment (xvii. 31). The
vital import of the fact and not its exceptional
nature was that which was of primary moment.

We are not then justified either by reason
or by Scripture in assigning to miracles, and still
less to the record of miracles, a supreme power of
proof. But none the less they fulfil externally
an important function in the Divine economy.
They are fitted to awaken, to arouse, to arrest the
faith which is latent. They bring men who
already believe in GOD into His Presence. They
place them in an attitude of reverent expectation.
This they do both at the crisis of performance,
when their full character can be but imperfectly
apprehended, and even more decisively afterwards
when they are studied in their spiritual aspects.

For while, as has been already said, our general
conception of GOD will decide finally whether a

particular fact can be referred to Him, as an indication of His will for us, or not, the fact itself which is admitted as consistent with His attributes, in its immediate or final scope, will be able to (may it not be said, will of necessity ?) reveal to us something more of His Nature and modes of action. For it is wholly groundless to suppose that we can anticipate or discover of ourselves what we can feel to be true when it is made known to us. Our power of discovery is not a measure of our power of recognition.

In this relation it is of the utmost importance in studying the miracles of the Bible to observe the narrow limits of their occurrence, to note their absence from the history of particular periods and of particular men : to pay attention to the distinguishing character, the contrasts and correspondences, of groups of miracles : to consider their relation to the work and person of each Divine messenger. Whole structures of popular objections, for example, fall before a simple statement like that in which the Evangelist undesignedly contrasts the ministry of the Baptist with the ministry of Christ, 'John indeed did no sign' (John x. 41).

So, again, it will appear upon examination

that the miracles of the Lord are in fact a revelation of His Person, differing (as a whole) from
all other miracles in the mode of their accomplishment and in the completeness of their range.
Christ fulfilled His Works as in direct personal
fellowship with the Father by His own power.
He conveyed to others by His commission the
power of working like signs (Matt. x. 8; Luke
x. 9). And in the Gospels the record of these characteristic works appears as part of the ordinary
narrative. No emphasis is laid upon their significance, but at the same time it is indicated that
they were designed to cast light upon mysteries,
to be sacraments, as it were, of divine working, as
when the fact of the forgiveness of sin was illustrated by the healing of the paralytic (Matt. ix.
1 ff.).

And there is one special function which
'signs' were fitted to fulfil at the beginning of
the life of the Church. They set vividly before
the believers through whom they were wrought a
personal relation of God to themselves. In these,
if we may so speak, He was seen directly acting
with them. And this consideration helps us to
understand why 'signs' should be grouped together
at certain critical periods, and why at other times
they should not occur. If the sense of personal

communion with GOD is established, and exactly
in proportion as it is established, the tendency of
the believer will be to desire to rest more and
more absolutely in the hands of GOD, to shrink
from wishing in the least degree to modify what he
has learnt to apprehend as the general expression
of GOD's will. Under the action of such feelings
a miracle might become morally impossible not as
in other circumstances from want of faith but
from the energy of faith. An exceptional occurrence, an interruption of the order which has been
welcomed at last as the fulfilment of the divine
counsel, would not extend or deepen the sense of
divine fellowship, but even disturb and confuse it.

CHAPTER VIII.

As distinguished from all other religions
Christianity is *absolute* and *historical.* It claims
on the one side to be bound by no limits of
place or time or faculty or object, but to deal
with the whole sum of being, and with the whole
of each separate existence. It claims on the
other side to give its revelation in facts, which
are an actual part of human experience, so that
the peculiar teaching which it offers as to the
nature and relations of GOD and man and the
world is simply the interpretation of events in the .
life of men and in the Life of One Who was truly
Man.

There is indeed an apparent contradiction
in these two attributes. It is customary to
oppose the 'absolute' to the 'historical,' just as

the 'abstract' is opposed to the 'concrete.' But in
fact the combination indicates that Christianity
answers to both terms of the antithesis which
underlies all life.   The antithesis exists and
Christianity meets it.   Christianity announces in
the plainest terms a vital union of the finite
and the infinite as the fundamental Gospel.   In
the brief phrase *'the Word became flesh'* the
opposition and the reconciliation, the difference
and the union in one Person, of Being eternal
and temporal, is set forth not as a speculation
or as a thought, but as a historic event.

In order to understand what Christianity
claims to be, it will therefore be necessary to
examine these complementary characteristics of
its nature.

Christianity claims to be absolute.   It claims
to extend without distinction to all men, to the
whole of man, to all being, and to all time.

Christianity claims to extend to all men.
This claim is correlative to the Christian postulate
as to man's creation in the image of GOD (Gen. i.
27).   In spite of all differences between man and
man, however induced, this inward identity of
nature remains.   Men are alike so far as they are
akin to GOD; and the Gospel is addressed to
them as such.   And further men are alike in fact,

so far as they have fallen short of a standard
acknowledged by themselves (Rom. iii. 23). All
men, in other words, are capable of receiving the
divine message, and all men need the grace which
it offers.

This thought of the universality of the
Christian message is shadowed out in the begin-
nings of the Gospel, in the Song of Simeon (Luke
ii. 32; cf. Is. xlii. 6; xlix. 6), and in the Sermon
on the Mount. Christ is welcomed as *a light for
revelation to the Gentiles:* His disciples are pronounced by Him to be *the light of the world, the
salt of the earth* (Matt. v. 14, 13), the power which
shews finite being in its true beauty: the element
which keeps that which is corruptible from decay.
The boundaries of the Holy City and of Israel are
no longer as in old time the limits of the divine
Presence, and of the divine sovereignty, though
Christ Himself fulfilled His work within them.
That which was historically confined to one
scene in fulfilment of the laws of the divine
order was essentially universal. The crowning
sign of the Christ was the proclamation of a
Gospel to the poor (Matt. xi. 5)—to the poor in
the largest acceptation of the term, the poor in
means, in intellect, in feeling, all whom the world
holds to be weak. The stamp of universality was

first impressed upon the work, and then the work was wrought out, fragment by fragment, according to the circumstances of the time.

It could not but be necessary, in the order of Providence, that some little time should elapse before the absolute universality of Christianity, without regard to differences of sex, or race, or culture, or age, could find a clear and consistent enunciation in the preaching of the Apostles. But the doctrine did obtain at least a partial expression in the first proclamation of the Gospel on the Day of Pentecost. *The promise*, St Peter said to the inquiring multitude, *is to you and to your children and to all that are afar off, even all whom the Lord our* GOD *may call* (Acts ii. 39). Some indeed have supposed that these words refer only to different classes of the Jews, to the immediate hearers of the Apostles, to those who were nearest to them, and to their fellow-countrymen scattered among the nations. But such an interpretation seems to fall short equally of the elevation of the Apostle's language and of the prophecy on which he bases his address. According to the teaching of Joel, the restoration of Israel was the prelude and the pledge of the complete fulfilment of the purposes of GOD, but it was not itself the complete fulfilment (Joel ii. 32).

These words then cannot be justly regarded as ambiguous, and St Paul distinctly appeals to the same prophecy in order to shew that *there is no difference between the Jew and the Greek, for the same Lord over all is rich unto all that call upon Him* (Rom. x. 12, 13). Thus the oldest prophecy and the earliest preaching of the Gospel meet together and coincide in offering a universal promise of a spiritual kingdom as the final message of GOD. The ideal stands out in its full glory from the first. In later times men must go back that they may realise it little by little.

For we must go from St Peter to St Paul, from Jerusalem, the centre of the divine election, to Athens, the centre of human exclusiveness, to hear the statement of the universality of the Gospel made together with its essential justification. St Paul says, standing on the Areopagus, *GOD that made the world and all things therein,...made of one (ἐξ ἑνός not ἐξ ἑνὸς αἵματος) every nation of men...that they should seek the Lord...for in Him we live and move and have our being...The times of ignorance then GOD winked at, but now commandeth men that all everywhere should repent* (xvii. 24 ff.). In other words the Apostle declares the universality of the Gospel as corresponding with the original constitution and the actual condition of man. He was made by GOD, and for GOD; and he has missed the true end of his being as man, which is at last plainly set before him.

Elsewhere St Paul regards this universality from the opposite point of sight. The faith is universal not only in its destiny but also in its combining power: *Ye are all sons of GOD through the faith* (or your faith), [sons] *in Christ Jesus... There is no place* [in Him] *for Jew or Greek, there is no place for slave or free, there is no place for male and* (καὶ) *female. For ye all are one man— one person—in Christ Jesus* (Gal. iii. 26 ff.). Historical differences of race and class, and even the natural, fundamental (Gen. i. 27), difference of sex, are lost in a supreme unity and a perfect life.

And this unity, as St Paul teaches in a parallel passage (Col. iii. 10 f.), is the realisation of the type of creation. The new life, the new personality, with which men are invested in Christ, is *renewed* (comp. 2 Cor. iv. 16)—shaped little by little and day by day—*unto knowledge according to the image of Him that created him, where there is no place for Greek and Jew, circumcision and uncircumcision, barbarian, Scythian, slave, free, but Christ is all things and in all things.*

These three passages studied together present

in a few traits a complete vision of Christ's universal work for men as fulfilling the end of Creation. First there is the statement of GOD's purpose of love, of man's need, of the pledge of the possibility of redemption in man's true nature. Then follows the declaration of the union of believers in one Person (εἰς ἐστέ), by which our thoughts are raised to the contemplation of a vaster life than that which is realised individually, a life in which humanity becomes one, a life which is not an abstraction nor simply a participation in a common nature (ἕν ἐστε. Comp. St John x. 30), but (as we apprehend it) personal (comp. Eph. iv. 15 f.). And in the third place the life which has been regarded in its supreme unity in Christ is regarded, so far as this is possible, in its separate parts, '*ye are one man in Christ*'; and conversely '*Christ is all things and in all.*' The differences between man and man are in the faithful, partial manifestations of Christ. Whatever is, He is. There is but one life. And thus in the personal lives of Christians His image, the archetype of man as originally created, is more and more completely attained.

We are perhaps inclined to underrate the importance of this announcement in Christianity of the universal spiritual brotherhood of men. The

truth had indeed been set forth in the far East in
Buddhism, and it was (and is) the strength of
Buddhism. But in the West it was unknown as
a doctrine of religion. In Buddhism too the truth
was based upon a view of the world diametrically
opposed to the Christian view of the world. And
the philosophic universalism of the Stoics is
pathetic in its hopelessness as compared with
the teaching of these systems. The brotherhood
of men which the Gospel proclaimed was not
deduced from a view of the evils and vanities of
existence, or from the recognition of an inevitable
necessity. It was combined with the offer of the
eternal inheritance of sons. It was set forth as
revealing the glory of GOD. It was given as an
interpretation of the divine idea in creation
shaped before sin had entered into the world and
(as things are) established by the conquest of
sin.

The novelty of the Christian doctrine is seen
in this view which the Apostle gives of the correspondence of creation and redemption. The
Gospel was addressed to all men, and potentially
it availed for all men: *as in Adam all die, so
also in Christ shall all be made alive* (1 Cor. xv.
22). The new creation is, in one sense, presented
as coextensive with the old creation. The victory

of Christ is declared by St Paul to compensate for
and to outweigh the fall of Adam; and this truth
is affirmed in various ways in each group of the
apostolic writings.   It must be enough to indicate
some representative passages:

(1) *Synoptic Group.*

1 Pet. ii. 9 f.
   The mixed body a spiritual Israel.
   The condition of fellowship, faith (*v.* 6).
   Extending potentially to Gentiles: *v.* 12.
   even to the dead: iv. 6.

(2) *The Epistles of St Paul.*

1 Cor. xv. 22.
1 Cor. xv. 45.
Rom. v. 12 ff. ἐφ᾽ ᾧ for that (2 Cor. v. 4): πάντας
   comp. xi. 32.
      14. ὅς ἐστι τύπος τοῦ μέλλοντος.
      15. ὁ εἷς—οἱ πολλοί. ἐπερίσσευσεν.
      19. ὁ εἷς—οἱ πολλοί. κατασταθήσονται
         οἱ πολλοί.
Eph. i. 10.
Col. i. 20.

(3) *The writings of St John.*

1 John ii. 2.
Apoc. v. 9.

Compare John i. 29; iii. 17; vi. 51; John xii. 32 (notice πάντα אD Latt.).

It does not concern us now to consider how the hope indicated in these passages can be realised. It is probably impossible for man ever to comprehend in the existing order of things how the divine purpose attains its full completion. All that requires to be observed at present is, as I have said, the novelty of this Christian conception of a universal brotherhood, in which a definite fact is treated as the sufficient bond of humanity. And while the thought is unique, it answers to the aspirations of men. There is that in us which points to a vital fellowship, fulfilled personally, as the one issue in which our fragmentary lives can find their consummation. In this respect the Gospel, the record of the new Creation, corresponds with the record of the first Creation. The unity shewn in the beginning is established at the end.

Christianity claims in this way to deal with all men. It claims also to deal with the whole of man. It claims to preserve and to perfect each part in his complex nature. Man, made in the image of GOD, is an indivisible being. We naturally, or even necessarily, speak of 'body' and 'soul' in such a way as to imply that man's soul is the real 'self,' complete and separable from his 'body.' Yet careful reflection will shew that such language simply expresses an abstraction. There is undoubtedly an antithesis in man, an organism and something which works through the organism. But the living man, the self, is not a part of this antithesis: he consists in combination of both parts. He can no more conceive himself remaining without the one factor than without the other.

It is not necessary for us to enter on any discussion of the principles of biblical psychology. We may at once admit that, as far as the constitution of man falls within the range of his own observation, we have no more reason to expect to find in the Bible a revealed system of psychology than to expect to find there a revealed system of physics. But Scripture distinctly recognises different elements in man corresponding with his different relations to being, and leads us to look for the preservation of all in the future. It lends no support to the famous utterance of Plotinus, who thanked GOD that "he was not tied to an immortal body." It lends no support to the view that the body as such is a mark of the soul's fall. *May the GOD of peace himself,* St Paul writes in his earliest Epistle, *sanctify you wholly ; and may your spirit and soul and body*

*be preserved entire, without blame at the coming
of our Lord Jesus Christ. Faithful is He that
calleth you, who will also do it* (1 Thess. v. 23).

But it is unnecessary to pursue this doctrine
in detail so far as it is expressed or implied
in isolated texts. The doctrine is essentially
characteristic of Christianity as 'the Gospel of
the Resurrection.' The Resurrection of Christ,
the central fact which the Apostles were commis-
sioned to announce, presented the truth of the
permanence of the whole sum of human nature as
the one sufficient answer to man's questionings as
to the future life. The Apostles did not announce
any opinion or argument or revelation as to the
immortality of the soul: their first message to
the Jews on the day of Pentecost was: *This Jesus*
[whom ye crucified] *GOD raised up, whereof* (or *of
whom*) *we all are witnesses* (Acts ii. 32); and
the same event was everywhere afterwards set
forth as the foundation of warning and hope. No
theory was advanced as to the conditions of the
new life, or as to the physical continuity of man's
'spiritual' body with his 'natural' body. Such
questions are evidently beyond the reach of our
present faculties. But the whole apostolic Gospel
was inspired by the thought that the redemption
accomplished through Christ extended to every

part of man: that as Christ rose again, wholly the
same and yet wholly changed, so should it be with
those who believed in Him: nothing was to be
lost in the transition, but all was to be trans-
figured (2 Cor. v. 1 ff.; iii. 18; 1 Cor. xv. 35 ff.).
The thought thus presented was nowhere anticipated in Jewish or heathen teaching. By
binding the seen to the unseen in the unbroken
unity of the personal life of the Lord 'who was
dead and is alive' the Apostles offered to men a
new interpretation of human duty and human
destiny. How strange and far-reaching the truth
was can perhaps best be seen by comparing the
later partial and limited representations of it with
the original message; the maimed and mutilated
views of the offices of the present life which have
found acceptance from time to time, with the type
of a complete and glorified offering; the various
schemes of a future life which have been sketched
by the aid of pious imagination, with the fulness
of promise transcending definite thought which is
opened in the revelations of the Risen Christ.

The doctrine of the Resurrection which throws
a new light on the 'material' element in man,
the part which he has in common with the
material universe, necessarily places all creation
in a direct connexion with the fulness of man's

hope. · The body of man is bound, how closely we are slowly coming to know, with the world in which he lives. The assumption of this body of flesh by the Son of GOD offers therefore the thought of larger issues of the Incarnation than we apprehend at first. In this respect the message of Christianity corresponds with the earliest teaching of Genesis on the Creation and the Fall. As the whole finite order received the same blessing as man, being pronounced "very good": as it afterwards shared in the consequences of his sin (Gen. iii. 17 f., comp. v. 29; Is. xxiv. 5, 6); so it is destined to share in the glory of his restoration. This cardinal truth is shadowed out in the word with which the Lord describes the period of His reign: *the regeneration* (ἡ παλιγγενεσία)— the new order which issues from a new birth (compare Rom. viii. 22, συνωδίνει)—*when the Son of Man has taken His seat on the throne of His glory* ('His throne of glory' Matt. xix. 28; not in parallels). And at the very beginning of the apostolic work, when the first miracle of healing had revealed the visible power of *the name of Jesus Christ of Nazareth* (Acts iii. 6), St Peter points the people who listened to his interpretation of the sign to the certain coming of those *times of the restoration* (ἀποκατάστασις) *of all things* which had been from the first the subject of prophetic promise (Acts iii. 21: compare Acts i. 6; Matt. xvii. 11). The thought lies here perhaps in an undefined shape. In the teaching of St Paul it stands out in magnificent fulness. *The earnest expectation of the creation waiteth for the revealing of the sons of* GOD. *For the creation was subjected to vanity, not of its own will, but by reason of him who subjected it, in hope that the creation itself also shall be delivered from the bondage of corruption into the liberty of the glory of the children of* GOD. *For we know that the whole creation groaneth and travaileth in pain together until now. And not only so, but ourselves also, which have the firstfruits of the Spirit, even we ourselves groan within ourselves, waiting for our adoption, to wit, the redemption of our body* (Rom. viii. 19—23).

The thought expressed in these pregnant words is indeed contained in the Christian conception of man. He is sovereign of the world (Gen. i. 28; comp. ii. 19) and therefore incomplete without his dominion. So much we can see, though we are not yet able to grasp the complete meaning of the truth from our imperfect knowledge of the world and of the interdependence in coexistence or succession of the various parts of which it is composed.

But the general recognition of the reality of the indestructible bond between man and nature opens out new lines for the study of both. In this connexion the promise of the Lord as to the future recompense of His followers (Matt. xix. 29 and parallels), and the language of St Paul (1 Cor. iii. 22, 23) as to the sovereignty of believers gain a fuller meaning.

In the Apocalypse the restoration of man and the restoration of nature are placed side by side. The Christian seer uses the language of Isaiah when he portrays the consummation of the work of the Christ. He sees 'a new heaven and a new earth' (Apoc. xxi. 1; Is. lxv. 17; lxvi. 22; comp. li. 16), and adds to the vision a fresh trait: 'and the sea is no more,' the element of restless instability has at length passed away. 'Four living creatures,' the representatives of animate Creation join with 'four and twenty elders,' the representatives of the Church, old and new, in rendering adoration to Him 'that sitteth on the throne' (iv. 6 ff.). When the living creatures give 'glory and honour' to Him, the elders fall down and worship Him and say 'Worthy art Thou, our Lord and our GOD, to receive the glory and the honour and the power; for Thou didst create all things, and because of Thy will they

were, and were created' (iv. 11). The hymn of
nature is crowned by the message of revelation;
and for a moment we are allowed to look to the
archetypal thought of finite being before time was
($\mathring{\eta}\sigma\alpha\nu$: comp. Aug. *in Joh.* c. i. 3 f.). So it is that
when the angels sing of the triumphant redemp-
tive work of 'the Lamb that hath been slain'
(v. 12), 'Every created thing which is in the
heaven and on the earth and under the earth, ·
and on the sea, and all things that are in them'
join in the ascription of blessing to Him; 'and
the four living creatures said Amen; and the
elders fell down and worshipped' (v. 13 f.). The
triple homage of the universe is at length complete and harmonious.

It will be obvious how such aspects of nature
as those shadowed out in these last visions of the
world's re-creation, even as they are indicated in
the record of the first creation, fall in with much
popular speculation of our own time. Whether
the evidence on which theories of evolution are
maintained is at present adequate to support the
wide conclusions which are drawn from it or not;
whether indeed it is likely or not that conclusive
evidence on such a subject will ever be accumulated, may be fairly questioned; but there can
be no doubt that many independent lines of facts

converge towards the general view which represents the whole sum of finite being as united in a
continuous whole, of which the parts rise one
above another by indefinitely small gradations so
as to suggest the conception of an unbroken
succession.   And such a view, so far from being
inconsistent with what the Bible teaches us of
the world, does in fact fall in better with its
teaching, according to our present knowledge,
than the older view which regarded the action of
GOD as manifested intermittingly in successive
creative acts, and made sharp and abrupt separations between the different 'kingdoms' of nature.

If then we feel that the balance of evidence
favours the belief in the evolution of life, or more
truly of the organisms through which the life
reveals itself, according to the action of uniform
'laws,' we do not lose but gain by the conclusion.
The life of the whole world, if we dare so speak,
is thus presented to us in a form analogous to
that of the life of the individual man.   Little by
little our own completed organization grows from
the simplest germ by fixed 'laws,' but yet not
without GOD.   On this interpretation of the
'becoming' of the world the Microcosm answers
to the Macrocosm—man to the Universe—and
the mind can rest in moments of loftiest speculation on a reasonable thought of a supreme unity

of all finite being which falls under man's observation.

The Gospel carries this thought of unity
into a higher region. Just as man appears to
be a representative of the visible creation, so the
visible creation appears to represent the whole
finite order. When therefore *the Word became
flesh* he fulfilled the purpose of the Father *to sum
up all things in Christ* (ἐν τῷ Χριστῷ), *the things
in the heavens and the things upon the earth* (Eph.
i. 10). And, more than this, in consequence of
the ravages wrought by sin, it was *the good
pleasure of the Father through Him to reconcile
all things unto Himself, having made peace through
the blood of His cross; through Him, whether
things upon the earth or things in the heavens* (Col.
i. 19 f.). Thus we are taught that by the Incarnation all orders of finite being are brought to
their consummation in a divine harmony (compare Rom. xi. 36 ; 1 Cor. iii. 21 ff.; 2 Cor. v. 17 f.;
Eph. iii. 9, iv. 10 ; Phil. iii. 21 ; 1 Cor. xv. 27 f.).

It is obvious that these passages of Holy
Scripture open before us a prospect of mysteries
which we cannot distinctly realise. They shew
us one side—the divine side—of being. There is
also the human side, on which we recognise the

terrible law of the permanence of evil and its
productiveness. We may not forget that. But
at least this divine prospect is one on which we
shall do well to linger. It is not sharp enough
for dogmatism, but it is luminous enough for
hope. It reveals to us, if *through a glass* and
in a riddle, how the varied developments of lives
fragmentary and marred, of powers misused or
wasted, as far as we can trace their action, are
in the vision of the Apostle crowned with their
divine fulfilment. In this recognition of the
permanent connexion of man with nature, and of
the consequences which flow from it, we have
once again an example of those anticipations
in the Bible of later thoughts which bring
home to us the conception of its Inspiration. It
is not too much to say that the language of
St Paul could not have been understood, as we
can understand it, till our own generation. In
the slow advance of experience great questionings
are shaped, and then in due time we find that we
can read the answer to them in the apostolic
interpretation of facts which are felt to be fuller
and richer in their applications as our knowledge
of the conditions of our being becomes more
complete.

Christianity, which reaches in this way to

all finite being, claims also to be a final Revelation, to endure through all time and to 'be' beyond time. There can be no addition to that which is implicitly included in the facts of the Gospel. We can conceive nothing beyond the unity which they imply. The facts contain in themselves all that is slowly wrought out in thought and act until the consummation. In one sense all has been done: in another sense much remains to be done. But from first to last One sovereign Person is present, who came and comes and will come, the beginning and the end (Apoc. xxii. 13; Matt. xxviii. 20; Acts i. 11).

It must be evident from this rapid summary that the claims of Christianity as an absolute religion are unique. It claims to bring the perfection no less than the redemption of finite being. It claims to bring a perfect unity of the whole sum without destroying the personality of each man. It claims to deal with all that is external as well as with all that is internal, with matter as well as with spirit, with the physical universe as well as with the moral universe. It claims to realise a re-creation coextensive with creation. It claims to present Him who was the Maker of the world as the Heir of all things, and entering on His inheritance (Hebr. i. 2). It claims

to complete the circle of existence, and shew how
all things came from GOD and go to GOD (Rom.
xi. 36; 1 Cor. xv. 28).

And it is of great importance to observe that
essentially these claims of Christianity are in a
large degree independent of the intrusion of sin
into the universe. Even if there had been no
separation of man from GOD, no disorder in the
physical universe, man, as far as we can see,
could not have attained his possible consummation, nor the dispersed creation its final unity,
without some such manifestation of Divine love
as the Gospel announces.

There are now, as there always have been,
partial interpretations of Christianity which gain
currency according as they meet individual or
local or temporal peculiarities. According to
some the essence of Christianity lies in the fact
that it is the supreme moral law. According to
others its essence is to be found in true doctrine,
or more specially in the scheme of redemption, or
in the means of the union of man with GOD.
Christianity does in fact include Law, and Doctrine, and Redemption, and Union, but it combines
them all in a still wider idea. It establishes the
principle of a Law, which is internal and not
external, which includes an adequate motive for

obedience and coincides with the realisation of freedom (James i. 25). It is the expression of the Truth, but this Truth is not finally presented in thoughts but in facts, not in abstract propositions but in a living Person. It is a scheme of Redemption, but it has relations also to man as he was created and not only to man fallen. It is a power of Union, but this Union transcends the range of humanity, and opens before the believer visions of glory which his thought cannot adequately coordinate or define.

In this then lies the main idea of Christianity, that it presents the redemption, the perfection, the consummation of all finite being in union with GOD. No doubt such a conception is too vast for man to keep constantly before him in a practical shape, but it is necessary both for strength and for progress that he should dwell upon it, and not acquiesce in any partial interpretation of the scope of the Gospel.

'And though the contemplation of it may be 'without the range of the personal teaching of 'Christianity which commonly limits our religious 'thought, yet it is a duty to strive, as occasion 'may arise, to grasp the full proportions of the 'hope which it brings to man and to the world. 'It is not always enough that each should feel in

'his own heart the power of the Gospel to meet
'individual wants.   We must claim for it also to
'be recognised as a wisdom revealed and realised
'only in the advance of time, and embracing in
'one Infinite Fact all that men have aspired to for
'themselves and for the transitory order in which
'they are placed.'

It is only in this way that we can intelligently
follow and understand the course of Christian
history : it is only in this way that we can observe
proportion in dealing with the problems of our
own time.

For as the idea of Christianity is unique and
absolute, so also is the fact in which the idea is
presented.   The announcement that *the Word
became flesh* (ὁ λόγος σὰρξ ἐγένετο) is wholly
unapproached in earlier religious speculations or
mythologies.   When a recent writer says : 'It is
'quite true that a decided step beyond the doc-
'trine of Philo is made when the Logos is repre-
'sented as σὰρξ ἐγένετο in the person of Jesus,
'but this argument is equally applicable to the
'Jewish doctrine of wisdom, and that step had
'already been taken before the composition of the
'[Fourth] Gospel,' he seems to me to miss the
whole meaning of the Incarnation.   There is, as

far as I can see, no real likeness between the intellectual process by which the Divine Wisdom came to be regarded (in some sense) as personal, and the assertion that historically the Word became flesh. The essence of the idea of the Incarnation lies not in the recognition of a distinct divine person, but in the personal and final union of the Godhead and humanity. There had been real theophanies under the old dispensation in which GOD had been pleased to manifest Himself under a limited and transitory form. There had been fabled theophanies in the mythologies of the East and West, in which gods were said to have assumed for a time, and as a veil, the form of men, or even of lower creatures, for purposes of mercy, or judgment, or caprice, or passion. There had been fabled apotheoses in which heroes had laid aside their dress of mortality and gained entrance into the family of heaven. But the assumption of humanity, not for a time, but for ever, by the Word, who is GOD, was a truth undreamt of till it was realised. And yet it answers to the original constitution of man's nature. If he was made capable of union with GOD, to which truth his aspiration towards GOD is a silent and lasting witness, the consequence seems inevitable that this union would be brought about; and this (as far as our thoughts reach)

could only be by GOD freely taking, not a man,
but humanity, to Himself.

Thus we return to the point from which we
started. The first Gospel lies in the record of
Creation (Gen. i. 27). It was given before the
Fall and not after the Fall. The Divine counsel
of the union of GOD with man realised in the
Incarnation is the foundation of Revelation. The
poverty and sorrow and passion of Christ were
due to sin, but we dare not suppose that the
consummation of the destiny of humanity was
due to such a cause. The thought reaches to the
very foundations of our Faith. Perhaps we may
add that now at last it falls in with the peculiar
conditions of our knowledge and our difficulties.
So at last our Theology gains a transformation
like that which was achieved in astronomy by
the conception of Copernicus; it becomes Theo-
centric, while before it was anthropocentric: the
ruling idea is not the self-assertion of man but
the loving will of GOD.

CHAPTER IX.

CHRISTIANITY HISTORICAL.

WE have seen that Christianity claims to be absolute, to extend without limit to all men, to the whole of man, to all being, to all time, or rather to eternity. At the same time since revelation comes through life and stands in a vital connexion with the whole life of humanity it must be progressive or apprehended progressively. Christianity therefore claims also to be historical; and by this claim it is distinguished from all other religions. Its teaching, its life, its essence is a history. It was prepared by a long national development, into which the typical elements of the ancient world entered as contributory forces. It is summed up in the facts of a divine-human life. It has been, and still is being, wrought out in the slow and unreturning growth of a society.

In this sense Christianity is the only historical

religion. There is a sense in which Christianity and Mohammedanism, for example, may be classed together as historical religions, so far as the facts connected with the personality and life of their Founders, their origin and progress and development, can be traced in documents which are adequate to assure belief. But it is not in this sense primarily that Christianity is historical. Christianity is historical not simply or characteristically because Christ standing out before the world at a definite time and place proclaimed certain truths and laid down certain rules for the constitution and conduct of a society. It is historical because He offered Himself in His own Person, and He was shewn to be in the events of His Life, the revelation which He came to give. It is historical in itself, in its essence, and, this being so, it is, in a secondary and yet in a unique sense, historical in its antecedents and in its realisation.

Christianity is historical in its antecedents. It is the fulfilment of Judaism, which was in its very idea definitely prospective, and only really intelligible through the end to which it led. The Covenant with Abraham included the promise of which the later religious history of 'the people,' working throughout for and in 'the nations,' was

the gradual accomplishment. The call of Abraham
was the beginning of the universal life of Faith.
For as Christianity was the goal of the revelations of the Old Testament, so it was also the
answer to the questions of the whole præ-Christian world, the satisfaction of the aspirations of
the 'many nations' with whom in the order of
Providence the 'people' was brought into contact.

Christianity is historical in itself. It is not a
code of laws: it is not a structure of institutions :
it is not a system of opinions. It is a life in
fellowship with a living Lord. The Work and
the Person of Christ, this is the Gospel, both
as it was proclaimed by the Lord Himself, and
as it was proclaimed by His Apostles : the revelation, the gift, the power, of a perfect human
life offered to GOD and received by GOD, in and
with which every single human life finds its
accomplishment. The laws, the institutions, the
opinions, of Christendom are the expression of the
life which works through them. In Christianity
the thoughts by which other religions live are
seen as facts.

Christianity is also historical in its realisation.
All human experience must be a commentary on

the perfect human Life. The new life which was communicated to men requires for its complete embodiment the services of all men. The fuller meaning of the Faith in Him Who is the Way and the Truth and the Life is slowly mastered through the ages by the ministry of nations and by the ministry of saints and heroes through which the thoughts of the nations are interpreted. Such a process must go on unhastingly, unrestingly, irreversibly to the end of time; and if anything can make us feel the nobility of life, it must be that in Christ we are enabled to recognise in the whole course of history a majestic spectacle of the action of Divine love in which no failures and no wilfulness of men can obliterate the signs and the promises of a Presence of GOD.

(i) *Christianity is historical in its antecedents.*

These general statements require to be presented somewhat further in detail.

Christianity is historical in its antecedents: it is the fulfilment of Judaism, the goal of the revelations of the Old Testament. The fact has been denied and misinterpreted from the first age to the present; but it is essential to the right understanding of the relation of revelation to life. It is affirmed in the plainest terms by the Lord, and it underlies all the teaching of the Apostles. The Apostles everywhere assume the continuity of their religious faith, even as the Lord *grew and waxed strong, becoming full of wisdom* (Lk. ii. 40, 51 f.) under the influence of Jewish teaching. All is summed up in the words: *Think not that I came to destroy (καταλῦσαι) the law or the prophets*—the outward discipline of ritual and rule by which Israel was moulded, and the spiritual promises by which Israel was quickened—*I came not to destroy, but to fulfil* (Matt. v. 17), to realise perfectly that to which they pointed, to abrogate the service of the letter and form only by taking it up without loss into a more perfect order. That to which the Levitical system witnessed as the supreme privilege of man—direct communion with GOD— given under typical ordinances to one man on one day in the year became in the Son of man the right of every Christian at all times (Hebr. iv. 16; x. 19 ff.; compare Lk. xvi. 17, xxii. 16; Matt. xxiii. 2 f., xxiv. 20).

So it is that in the Fourth Gospel—the Gospel of the Christian Church—words of the Lord have been preserved in which He marked the connexion in which He stood with the history

and with the institutions of the Old Covenant,
with Abraham (viii. 56; comp. i. 51), with Moses
(iii. 14, v. 46, vi. 31 ff.; vii. 22), with the Psalm-
ist (x. 34, xiii. 18, xv. 25). Nor is it too
much to say that all that is written out at
length in the Epistle to the Hebrews is implied
in these and other like pregnant sentences, in
which the believer recognises point by point
that *the salvation* in which he rejoices *is of the
Jews* (iv. 22 ἡ σωτηρία ἐκ τῶν Ἰουδαίων ἐστίν),
the fruit and not the perpetuation of the discipline of a people of GOD.

For however great uncertainty may still hang
over the details of Old Testament history, the
history of the Jews is, in its broad and unquestionable outlines, the history of a people who
believed, and who, with all their failures and
relapses, lived as believing in the intercourse
of GOD and man: who believed in the kinsman-
ship of men as made by GOD for His glory: who
believed in the righteous sovereignty of GOD,
guiding the affairs of the world to an issue corresponding with the purpose of Creation. From
first to last, so far as their faith found more
and more an articulate expression, the Jews
believed and lived as believing that they were
called to be witnesses to GOD as the Creator

17—2

and Preserver, the King and the Redeemer of all men.   .

This sublime faith is recorded in the series of Covenants which are an epitome of the history of præ-Christian revelation as it was interpreted by the prophets of Israel. The nature-covenant with Noah confirms the promise of Creation in spite of the sin by which the works of GOD have been marred. The grace-covenant with Abraham discloses the Divine counsel for guiding humanity to its true goal by the ministry of faith, effective through the service of one for all the nations of the earth. The work-covenant of Sinai brings to light the duty and the weakness of men, their social unity, the calling of a people. The life-covenant with David points forward to the future unity of 'the people,' and of 'the nations' through 'the people,' in One Who is 'the Son of GOD.' The whole history gives a view of the redemption and consummation of mankind through the realisation of the idea of holiness as the condition of that fellowship of man and men with GOD, for which they were made (Lev. xi. 44).

For while Israel was consecrated to GOD it was as 'a kind of firstfruits of His creatures.' The

whole people was regarded as being at once His
son (Ex. iv. 22; Hos. xi. 1), and His bride (Hos. ii.
14 f.; Jer. ii. 2 f.), an offspring and a source of
Divine life.   The work of Israel was not for itself
alone.   Every gift, every privilege, every lesson,
was to be used for others.   The popular view
of the exclusiveness of Israel is the exact opposite
of the truth.   The exclusiveness of the people
was the condition of its work, its life, but the
life was offered to all, with significant exceptions,
on the acceptance of the condition (Deut. xxiii.
3 ff., 7 ff.)   From the first provision was made for
the incorporation of strangers into the holy people
(Ex. xii. 38, 48; Lev. xxiv. 10; Num. xi. 4).
The terms of complete fellowship were fixed
not by descent but by character determined by
outward ordinances in an outward organisation.
Israel was a Messianic people, called to its office
not for any exceptional merits of its own but as
an instrument through which God was pleased
to accomplish His will for all His children.   Over
against stands Babylon the symbol of man's self-
deification.   Israel was to the nations, what priests
and prophets were to Israel, a witness of the
Divine claims on man and of the Divine purpose
for man.

In this respect Israel offers a sharp contrast

to the 'nations.' In Heathendom we follow what
we can understand as a natural development of
the powers of man, whether dominated by physical
forces from without, or by intellectual and moral
forces from within. But Israel grows under constraint. The Bible is full of the relapses of the
people. They are, from first to last, 'rebellious
and stiffnecked.' But the Lord subdues and
trains them, moving among them so that His
awful presence can be felt. The seriousness of
the Jew is a reflection of this Divine communion.
No præ-Christian literature offers anything which
can be compared with the sustained and most truly
human solemnity and grandeur of the Psalter.
The thoughts are the fruit of discipline.

In order to fit the people for the fulfilment
of this unique office they were placed in what
they felt to be a direct fellowship with GOD.
Their relation to Him was not abstract and
intellectual, but living and personal. They were
subjected to His discipline, that they might be
brought more and more into conformity with
Himself (Deut. viii. 2). And under this aspect
the successive stages in the history of Israel
are seen to be parts of an intelligible education,
tending to shape and fix a national character to
which the world offers no parallel. For the faith

of Israel was grounded not so much upon definite teaching as upon the facts, the experiences, of their life.

We have then in the Old Testament, to gather up most briefly what has been said, the representative record of the Divine discipline of a chosen people. In this history we are allowed to contemplate the clear signs of the action of GOD, and by the help of the lesson all history is felt to be the fulfilment of one eternal purpose.

Each great nation had and still has its peculiar work. The work of the Jews was to receive, to appropriate, to hand down a revelation of GOD. They learnt to know Him not as an abstract object of thought, not as dwelling in a distant heaven, not as reserving His sovereignty for a remote future; but as actually present with them in the business of daily life, making Himself felt in acts even more than in words, vindicating His character in judgments and mercies.

Their life and their hope lay alike in realising that the Lord was dealing with them from day to day. This was enough for their training. To us as we look back the details of their discipline suggest many further thoughts. Some even in old times may have grasped these thoughts by faith. But it does not concern us to attempt to determine how far this was so. The Law accomplished its office (Gal. iii. 24). Fenced in by its stern provisions the people were prepared during a long childhood for the duties of mature age.

The central moral idea which they were thus enabled to define and strive after, even through all failings, was holiness. The idea in its full scope corresponds with the final harmony of man's whole nature. It was offered to the world, it was recognised as the one sufficient end of being, it was found to be beyond human reach, before it was realised in Christ.

Thus the Jewish Dispensation could only find its consummation in one way. It dealt with that which was essentially human, and still in form it was limited and local. The revelation which it embodied was true but not final. It was from first to last a prophecy leading onwards to an issue which seemed at each successive stage to become more indispensable than before and more beyond hope. As we look back we can now see how one Presence and not only one increasing purpose is everywhere found in the Law and in the Prophets. The fathers found refreshment in the wilderness from the streams which flowed from the stricken rock. But far more than this: they drank living waters from a Rock not material but spiritual, from a Rock not fixed and im-

movable but which kept close to their wandering
feet, and that Rock was Christ (1 Cor. x. 4). The
prophets understood imperfectly the last meaning
of the words which they used, but 'the spirit
'of Christ which was in them testified before-
'hand the sufferings that should come unto
'Christ and the glories that should follow them'
(1 Pet. i. 11). From first to last, throughout
the long ages of preparation and onwards still till
the last vision of the growing Truth be gained,
the words of the angel in the Apocalypse hold
good, "The testimony of Jesus is the spirit of
prophecy" (Apoc. xix. 10). The witness to a
historic human Saviour, come and coming, is the
one unceasing message of GOD to man, the one
sure sign of inspiration (1 John iv. 2 f.).

ii.   *Christianity historical in its essence.*

Christianity is the goal of Judaism. Thus
we come to that which is the centre and source
of all Christian thought and life. For Christianity, as we have seen, is absolute as well as
historical; and the Incarnation connects and
reconciles the one characteristic with the other.
The Incarnation is a historic fact in the experience
of time, and it is an absolute truth in the counsel

of eternity. This fact, realised in fragments, is the Gospel.

Christ declared to us truths about the nature and the will of *His Father and our Father, His God and our God,* about human relationships and responsibilities, about man's worth and destiny, which it concerns us most deeply to know; but He did not come simply to lay down a system of doctrine.

He gathered into a brief compass and without admixture of alloy the noblest rules for life: He placed them in a natural connexion with the fulfilment of the simplest offices of common duty: He gave them, so to speak, a natural universality which man as man can at once acknowledge: He embodied them in an example which no lapse of time or change of circumstances can make less supreme in its attractiveness; but the Sermon on the Mount is neither the essence of His message to the world, nor, except incidentally, characteristic of it. The years which He passed in silence and obscurity, the months which He passed in teaching and reproof and discipline, are not, when regarded from without, the sum of His revelation.

The claim which He made for Himself and the claim of the first preachers, as of preachers in every age, was not primarily that men should

believe Him, or obey Him, or love Him, but that
they should believe in Him, that they should
recognise in Him a new source of power and life,
by which obedience · becomes possible and love
becomes energetic, and so throw themselves wholly
upon Him and enjoy fellowship with the fulness
of His glorified Being.

This unique claim is presented naturally, so
to speak, under such circumstances and in such
a form as to make its purpose and its effect
historically intelligible. The 'signs' which the
Lord wrought, and the teaching which He gave
tend to the same conclusion.

Christ's signs are distinguished as a whole
from all other wonderful works of His predecessors or followers, in the mode of their working,
and in their individual character, and in relation
to His whole redemption work (Matt. viii. 17),
and raise and answer thoughts in many hearts.
His words fix attention on Himself as being
more than His teaching; and taken in their due
succession as they have been recorded for us,
they give a summary of His self-revelation.

What He did and what He said alike constrains us to turn for the secret of His message to
what He was.

Christianity, to speak summarily, rests on the conviction that in the Life and Death and Resurrection of Christ something absolutely new and unparalleled has been added to the experience of men, something new objectively and not simply new as a combination or an interpretation of earlier or existing phenomena: that in Christ heaven and earth have been historically united: that in Him this union can be made real through all time to each believer: that His Nature and Person are such that in Him each man and all men can find a complete and harmonious consummation in an external order. The Life of Christ is something absolutely unique in the history of the world, unique not in degree but in kind. It is related to all else that is unfolded in time as birth, for example, is related to the development of the individual.

It is necessary that we should reflect upon these peculiar features of our Faith in order that we may understand the teaching of the New Testament, and the history of the Christian Church. All objections to the Gospels which are drawn from the exceptional or unparalleled character of the events which it affirms or implies are irrelevant. The Gospel is a Gospel because it is the proclamation of that which is new in human

experience, the Incarnation of the Word of GOD.
By the announcement of this fact it lays open
the unseen about us, and thus quickens and
supports the energy of Faith (Hebr. xi. 1): it
brings the sure promise of unity to all finite
things, and thus satisfies the aim of Religion
(Eph. i. 10; Col. i. 20): it reveals GOD so that
we can approach Him with confidence under the
forms of our human thought and feeling (John
xiv. 9 ff.): it illuminates the dark places of the
world so that we can look upon the chequered
scenes of man's failure and sin and suffering
without dismay (1 Cor. xv. 24 ff.).

Christ, to recapitulate in the shortest phrase
what has been said, the Incarnate Word, Son of
GOD, and Son of Man, is Himself in a most
true sense the Gospel.

Viewed in this light the Gospel of *the Word
become flesh* brings such an answer as we need,
and as we are able to receive, to the riddles
of life which widening experience proposes to us.
We readily admit that we are not able to grasp
completely or to systematise exactly the whole
Truth which is presented to us.   But we can
see, with sufficient clearness to gain confidence
in our work, that it throws light on the darkest
mysteries of self and the world and GOD.

It shews us, to repeat a little more fully what
has been already summarised, that we are not
isolated units but parts of that one humanity
which GOD made in His image to gain His likeness and which the Son of GOD, who became
Son of man, has raised beyond the heavens in
His body of glory: that we are enabled here to
gain our freedom and realise our personality by
fellowship with our Head: that every sorrow and
pain is an element of discipline, and that the
just anger of GOD is the other side of His sovereign love: that nothing is lost of that which is
revealed to us now under the conditions of sense,
when the limitations of sense cease to be.

It shews us that in the consummation of man
lies also the consummation of all created things:
that there is not one lost good, or one lost pang,
for all good is of and in Him who cannot change,
and every pang answers to His law whose wisdom
and mercy meet in righteousness: that the lesson
of our intimate connexion with material things
is not that we must be stripped of our spiritual
glory, but that we must gladly learn to recognise
in them unsuspected potentialities of a higher
destiny.

It shews us that we can approach GOD with
confidence under the forms of human thought
and feeling, not with a part of our nature only

but with the entire sum of our energies and powers: that outward phenomena are, as it were, the words in which He speaks to us, disclosing as we can understand them the thoughts which lie behind, representing but not exhausting them: that, in a sense which gives confidence to prayer and vigour to action and assurance to hope, *in Him we live and move and have our being.*

The unchangeable sum of Christianity is the message: *The Word was GOD, and the Word became flesh.* This being so, it is clear that Christianity is not essentially a law for the regulation of our conduct: not a philosophy for the harmonious coordination of the facts of experience under our present forms of thought: not a system of worship by which men can approach their Maker in reverent devotion. It offers all these as the natural fruit of the Truth which it proclaims in the Incarnation and Resurrection of Christ. But Christ Himself, His Person and His Life, in time and beyond time, and not any scheme of doctrine which He delivered, is the central object and support of Faith.

An examination of the earliest records of the Christian Faith will prove, as I hold, beyond question that this was the general view of the Gospel which was taken from the first: that this was the general view to which the Lord Himself guided His disciples in His preparatory teaching. Such lessons indeed were not learnt at once. They are not fully learnt even now. Each age has its own task, and we can dimly see our own. For Christianity, which is historical in its antecedents and in itself, is historical also in its realisation.

(iii) *Christianity historical in its realisation.*

From the first the Gospel was realised in the way of life. Little by little, the revelation of Christ's Nature was made through the events of His intercourse with men. The facts were open before the world: it was for those to whom they were made known to read their lessons. These were seen; and they were 'allowed to work.' In this respect the answer which the Lord gave to the disciples of the Baptist shews the manner of Revelation for all time. He sent no direct reply to His herald, but He stated plainly, and in a significant order, the signs from which the reply could certainly be deduced (Matt. xi. 2 ff.).

This characteristic of the method of Revelation is signally illustrated by the records of the Resurrection. The incidents preserved by the

Evangelists present two distinct and complementary views of the event. In one group we
have the assurance that the Risen Lord was
indeed the same Lord as the disciples had known
in His earthly life: in the other group we see
that He was raised above the conditions of earthly
existence. Either group by itself would be
wholly inadequate to convey the truth which
was to be made known. The first group alone
could only establish a rising again as that of
Lazarus to a life subject as before to death.
The second group alone would leave us in the
presence of shadowy, phantom-like appearances,
and offer no real connexion between the two
worlds. But the Evangelists give both groups
without any consciousness of an opposition and
without any direct interpretation. They present
Christ as wholly the same and yet wholly changed.
The significance of the two series of manifestations
in combination becomes apparent upon reflection;
and faith by a spiritual synthesis apprehends the
fact of a continuity of human life under new
conditions, of the transfiguration of all that
belongs to the fulness of humanity. By the
Resurrection of Christ thus realised the two
worlds—the seen and the unseen—are brought
into a union of life, and we see that the fact is
a revelation.

W. G. L.   18

The revelation was thus made through a succession of facts, and the import of the facts was historically apprehended by progressive thought. This is true in different ways both of the Apostles and of later Christian teachers; and the recognition of the truth is important for ourselves. For example, we commonly lose much by failing to notice how the Divine nature of Christ was slowly discerned under the action of (what we call) natural historical circumstances. It is assumed that all was clear from the first; and that the Apostles were enabled at once and finally to grasp the fulness of the revelation, and to regard Him with whom they had 'gone in and out' as being what St John in the end was enabled to declare Him to be, '*the Word become flesh.*'

Such a view is equally at variance with the method of Divine Providence, as made known to us in Scripture, and with the laws of the human mind. There is an order, a growth, in the teaching of GOD. This we know through our own experience. All indeed lies enfolded in the earliest seed but the actual development is to our observation slow and continuous and in successive phases.

The example of the great confession of St Peter at Cæsarea Philippi—the crisis in the historical ministry of Christ—is an illustration of this law. To us, with our preconceptions, such a confession seems to be the necessary expression of the effect which the Lord's works and words must have made upon all the disciples. The Lord's own judgment lays open our error. What is clear to us could be seen by the Apostles only through a Divine illumination which came in due time (Matt. xvi. 16 ff.; Mark viii. 29; Luke ix. 20 f.). And even so the full import of the inspired words was not firmly seized. The confession remained as a sign for later interpretation.

The sequel of the history itself shewed this. St Peter emboldened, if we may so speak, by the Lord's words sought shortly afterwards to fix the consequences of the confession which he had made and went wholly astray (Matt. xvi. 22 f.; compare on another side Matt. xvii. 24 ff.); and even afterwards the sons of Zebedee held scarcely less false views of what the end would be (Matt. xx. 20 ff.)[1].

[1] It is most instructive in this respect to study each confession of Christ recorded in the Gospels in connexion with the circumstances to which it belongs. Nathanael [St Bartholomew], St Peter, Martha and St Paul, each declared Jesus to be 'the Son of God' (John i. 49; Matt. xvi. 16; John xi. 27; Acts ix. 20), but each repetition of the words marked a distinct victory of faith. Compare also Mark i. 24 with John vi. 69; John i. 42, 46 with Matt. xvi. 20; and see John iv. 42; xvi. 30; xx. 28; xxi. 17.

The different groups of books included in the New Testament shew on a large scale the gradual apprehension of this central truth of the Christian Faith. The great outlines are written in the first twelve chapters of the book of the Acts, and it would be difficult to find a more convincing proof of the contemporary origin of the record than the naturalness with which point after point is reached till the proclamation of St Paul marks the attainment of St Peter's confession by a new line of experience (Acts ix. 20 ἐκήρυσσεν τὸν Ἰησοῦν ὅτι οὗτός ἐστιν ὁ υἱὸς τοῦ θεοῦ). This outline is filled up in the Epistles of St James and St Jude and the Synoptic Gospels, and completed at a later time by the Epistles of St Peter, the Apocalypse and the Epistle to the Hebrews, in which we find how the Lord fulfilled the teaching of the Law and the Prophets as the Messiah. The Epistles of St Paul unfold on many sides the doctrine of the Ascended Christ. And finally St John in his Gospel and Epistles, writing from the bosom of the Christian Church, presents the crowning truth of the Incarnate Word, so that, to take one illustration, the Passion itself, seen in its true significance, becomes a revelation of kingly glory.

Such was the law in the apostolic age ; and

the same law finds fulfilment beyond the limits
of Scripture. The privilege which 'is eternal life'
is the progressive knowledge of GOD (John xvii.
3, ἵνα γινώσκωσιν [-ουσιν]; 1 John v. 20). Towards this we are charged to strive: to neglect
this is spiritual death. So it is that the history
of Christianity is the history of the slow and progressive efforts which have been made to gain and
to embody an adequate knowledge of Christ in the
fulness of His twofold Nature, of the eternal
revealed under the conditions of time, of the
earthly raised to the heavenly, of the harmony
that is established potentially between man and
humanity and GOD, under the continuous guiding
of the living Spirit.

It is undoubtedly a chequered and often a
sad history. The human organs often obey most
imperfectly the spirit which moves them. There
are times of torpor, of sloth, of disease in the
Body; but even so the spirit is not quenched.
There are fallings away, and dismemberments,
but even so an energy of reproduction supplies
the loss. Empires rise and pass away, but the
Church lives on, changed from age to age and yet
the same, gathering into her treasure-house all
the prizes of wisdom and knowledge, and gradually
learning more and more of the infinite import
and power of the Truth which she has to proclaim.

Under this aspect the history of the Christian Church is the history of the victories of the Risen Christ gained through the Spirit sent in His Name (John xiv. 26). Such a conception of the nature of the strange and magnificent spectacle which is opened before us in the progress of the Faith is alone sufficient to bring together the many contrasted parts of which it is composed into an intelligible unity, to give significance to manifoldness of form, to inspire the whole with the manifest power of one Life.

But when we speak of victories we imply resistance, suffering, loss: the triumph indeed of a great cause, but a triumph which has been gained through effort and sacrifice. And such in fact is the history which we have to follow in the records of Christianity. These offer to us a sad and yet a glorious succession of battles, often hardly fought and sometimes indecisive, between the new life and the old, the life wholly reconciled to GOD and the life broken and disordered, which is our natural heritage.

We know that the struggle thus begun can never be ended in this visible order, but we know also that Christ has brought within His sway from age to age ever more of the total powers of humanity and more of the fulness of the nature of the individual man. Each age has to sustain its own part of the conflict; and the retrospect of earlier successes gives to those who have to face new antagonists and occupy new positions, patience and the certainty of hope.

For in a peculiar sense all history from the day of Pentecost is a sacred history; even as all history is in one sense the fulfilment of a Divine plan. At the same time after the coming of Christ as before it we may distinguish two elements in the progress of humanity, the 'natural' unfolding of man's powers as he is, and the Divine disciplining of man towards the ideal for the attainment of which he was made. In the one we see a development generally controlled by GOD; and in the other an education directly inspired and guided by GOD. On one side we watch growth; on the other side we welcome salvation. But every ripe result of growth subserves the work of that society which is the firstfruits of created things.

Such general reflections will probably approve themselves as true as a mere abstract statement. They are however forced upon us with peculiar power if we compare the Christianity of to-day with the Christianity of some other period, with apostolic, or mediæval Christianity, or with the Christianity of the Reformation.

And the difference which strikes us is not that of uniformity in one age against variations in another, of purity against corruption, of energy against deadness. Wherever we look we see a struggle going on, life fulfilled through death; but the broad effect of popular thought, and hope and practice is changed from age to age. And the change is seen to be greater if we fix our minds on the specific thoughts and hopes and practices which were actually dominant at the contrasted epochs. How far removed, for example, many of the questions touched on in the Decrees of the Council of Trent, or the XXXIX. Articles, or the Westminster Confession, are from our interests: how much that moves us most deeply finds in them no notice.

Such a phenomenon can cause us no surprise now. We shall not desire to explain it away. No one, I imagine, would seriously hold that the doctrines of contemporary Romanism have been secretly taught from the days of the Apostles in an unbroken succession; or that the Gospel was corrupted from the close of the Apostolic age till the 16th century; or that necessary new truth was 'developed' as a permanent, fixed,

endowment of Christendom under infallible guidance. We see that a Divine life is manifested
more or less perfectly from age to age through
a Divine society; but the manifestation is not
the life. As the circumstances of men and
nations change, materially, intellectually, morally,
the life will find a fresh and corresponding expression. We cannot believe what was believed
in another age by repeating the formulas which
were then current. The greatest words change
in meaning. The formulas remain to us a
precious heritage but they require to be interpreted. Each age has to apprehend vitally
the Incarnation and the Ascension of Christ.

And here I would again insist upon the
enormous difference between the logical development of a doctrine, and the progressive
interpretation of a fact through experience.
The fundamental statement of a doctrine can
never be complete. Its original limitation must
impair the validity of the deductions which are
drawn from it with accumulated force from step
to step. But the fact finds its interpretation
through the fulness of life. One influence cor-
rects and completes another. And the record
of this progressive interpretation lies in Christian
history.

Christianity then while it is one cannot be uniform. The embodiment of the Truth in thought and practice from time to time must answer more or less completely to each age and race. Or, to put the truth in another form, each age and race has an office for the interpretation, the unfolding, of the Faith.

The Gospel is, in the fullest sense of the words, of life, in life, unto life (comp. Rom. xi. 36). As we learn more of man and more of nature we learn more of Christ in whom we still see the Father.

It is for this reason that the study of Church History, under its broadest aspect, is of especial value now. While we acknowledge that we are called upon to labour in an age of great and rapid changes, we do not shrink from the responsibility of still claiming for the Gospel sovereignty over all progress. And history justifies the claim. Thus then when once we can feel that faith in the risen Christ, as King and Redeemer, has not only conquered all opposing forces in each past crisis, but preserved in each case and incorporated into itself all that which gave real vitality to the opposition which it encountered, our own courage will be quickened. And if there are at present great and noble thoughts, certain and far-reaching facts, which have not been brought into harmony, or rather which have not been recognised as being in harmony with the Gospel of the Resurrection, we can welcome them and if need be wait. Perhaps we have not yet gained the point of sight from which they will be seen in due relation to the whole revelation hitherto made known to us. But even so, they have already called something to our minds which had been often overlooked. The King and the Redeemer is Creator also; and we are already beginning to apprehend how a larger unity than we have yet grasped may hereafter include the race and the world, and reconcile the general relations of both to GOD with the personal responsibility of each separate man.

CHAPTER X.

WE have seen that the Gospel is the message of a Life, that it was made known to us through life and that it has been apprehended throughout the ages and is still apprehended in life. It is a light to walk by and not simply to contemplate. How then, we ask, is it verified? How are we ourselves assured of its Truth? The verification of the Gospel answers to the communication and the interpretation of the Gospel. The verification of the Gospel is in and through life, the life of men and the life of each man. It is verified outwardly by the testimony of history: it is verified inwardly by the testimony of experience. Both forms of testimony are required for complete assurance. Without the inward experience we might hold as true that which would be to us as a beautiful picture: without the outward history we might yield to the fancies of undisciplined enthusiasm. When the voice of society expressed in history and the voice of the soul agree, we have the highest conceivable assurance of the truth of their message.

Before we indicate some features in this two-fold testimony, it will be well to notice yet again the grounds on which it is maintained that a revelation of some kind is antecedently probable on the assumptions which have been made. For the continuous and effective discipline of human thought and action man has need of progressive knowledge. Knowledge furnishes the materials which faith uses. But here a difference arises as to the subjects of which knowledge may be gained. Within obvious limits man may obtain by direct observation knowledge of himself and of the world. But if he is to know GOD, GOD must reveal Himself. And such a revelation is made possible by the constitution of man. The fact that he is conscious of the being of GOD implies the capacity of knowing Him with human knowledge. There is, as we have already noticed, a potential Gospel in the language of the earliest record of Creation, which declares that man was made 'in the image of GOD.' It is not indeed too much to say that the assurance of a revelation

of GOD to man is included in the ideas of GOD
and man. If the power to know GOD exists in
man, such an endowment contains the promise
that it will not be left idle. And on the other
side it is by intercourse with GOD that man
advances towards the Divine likeness.

These truths may be presented in another
light. Man is not a self-centred, self-directed,
independent unit. He is born a son, and that
in a twofold relation to the seen and the unseen.
He would cease to be human if he were not disciplined by the influences of society; and for the
complete unfolding of his powers as man he
requires the fellowship of GOD. He is a microcosm
in regard to the visible world : he is a reflection
of GOD in relation to invisible being. The
microcosm must be studied through the observation of the parts of the great whole of which it is
an epitome : the reflection must be kept fresh
and vivid by the presence of Him whom it represents.

Such considerations would have remained in
full force if man had continued to grow according
to the normal law of his being. But it is evident
that this development has been interrupted. The
illuminating, sustaining power of Divine fellowship

which would have been required by man as a
finite creature, has become yet more necessary
for man as a sinful creature.

This conclusion is pressed upon us with pathetic force by the facts of common experience.
We hold firmly to the belief that all being, all
life, is when rightly understood, a manifestation
of the counsel and nature of GOD.   This is what
we mean when we confess that He is the Creator
and Preserver of the world.   All Truth in other
words which is the foundation of religion, that is
all Truth, is Theology.   The idea of GOD enters
into it and supports it.   GOD is the source, the
agent, the end of all things (Rom. xi. 36).   The
conviction in its most general form is necessary
for the inspiration and guidance of labour.   By
the recognition of this Divine origin and destina-
tion of knowledge the idea of holiness consecrates
beauty, truth and goodness, and invests what is
in form transitory and limited with an eternal
meaning.

But while this is so, the phenomena which we
see superficially and for a brief space present
difficulties and apparent contradictions in the
way of the belief which we retain.   It has been
nobly said by one well fitted to bear the witness:
'If I looked into a mirror and did not see my
'face, I should have the same sort of feeling

'which actually comes upon me when I look into
'this living busy world and see no reflection of
'its Creator.'

So it is that in the actual state of man, the
revelation of GOD in the world without and in the
soul within is partially obscured and partially
defaced. This imperfection does not indeed alter
the essential character of the whole order of
things as fitted to make GOD known, or of the
soul as formed to recognise Him, but it leads us
to expect, as we believe in the government of GOD,
that some new light will be given to make our
way clear.

Man, in other words, conscious of disorder
within him and in the presence of a disordered
world, looks for some further revelation; a revelation through which he may be still enabled to
fashion the Divine image in which he was made
after the Divine likeness for which he was made:
a revelation which can be apprehended according
to the intellectual limitations of his nature, and
which can find expression in the language of men:
a revelation which takes account of other orders
of being but only so far as they come within the
moral scope of humanity; and yet more, a revelation which deals with man not as a stationary
being but as advancing with a continuous growth.

If then we assume that GOD governs the world which He made, and continues to regard man whom He formed in His own image, it follows that it is not only natural to look for such a revelation but that such a revelation is in itself most truly natural. It is most properly an unveiling of that which lies within the range of man's powers and which he was so made as to see in due time. It corresponds with what we conceive as the right development of man, according to the idea of creation. This development has unhappily been interrupted by a premature effort on man's part after independence and knowledge; but the sin of man has not fatally hindered the fulfilment of the Divine counsel.

We go on therefore to ask, How can we conceive such a revelation to be made? Briefly we reply it must come through life, interpreted by thought. It may be recorded in books after it has been realised in the vital processes of observation, reflection and action; but it passes from life into the record, and it is brought out of the record into life. It cannot be intellectual only. The first fact that it is the memorial of human experience is the pledge of the other, that it is available for man. Spiritual influences are transmitted normally from the whole person to the whole person. The truth which comes to man through natural human experience

can for that reason reach man fully (John v. 39 f.).
This being so, we can see that if in the conduct of
life we are enabled to see signs of the Divine government and counsel made plain, we have a revelation
which enlightens the dark places of the world
and sustains and directs faith; and we can see
that if we are allowed to contemplate and enter
into the realisation of a perfect human life
accepted by GOD, a life, that is, wrought out
under the conditions of earth in all its parts
and through death in perfect fellowship with
GOD, that will be for us a perfect revelation, a
revelation perfectly suited to our wants and to
our faculties.   And we can see further that such
a perfect revelation could not have been given in
the infancy of the race.   It could only come
naturally, that is in accordance with what we
observe of the Divine working, at the close of
a long preparatory discipline.

Such a revelation, made through life, gives us
facts and not formulated opinions.   Like observation in relation to the world of sense, it gives new
data.   These faith appropriates; and reason tests,
coordinates, adjusts them; for reason is critical
and formative and not creative.   Man by himself
cannot rise above himself: but he can use that
which will raise him.

In this way, as we believe, GOD has dealt with us. He has revealed Himself in life, and specially in the life of a chosen nation and in the Life of His Son. That which is of life reaches to life and the Truth which is embodied in Religion is not for speculation only or for contemplation only, but for life. It enlarges and harmonises knowledge, and it supplies a motive for effort. It appeals to head, heart, will; and it calls out understanding, feeling, action, in due proportion. So it is that it tends to bring perfect freedom (John viii. 32).

Knowledge, I have said, furnishes the materials which faith uses. The statement has a far-reaching application.

If we go back to the three fundamental conceptions, self, the world, GOD, we shall notice one feature that is common to them. In fashioning each we enter upon the future and the unseen, and act without hesitation on the conclusions which we have formed. We do not even pause to question the continuity of self, or of physical laws, or of character. We are so made as to draw from experience conclusions wholly beyond experience. Nothing in the observation of the past is in itself able to assure us as to what will be. The past can give no pledge that no new forces will be hereafter revealed, or that we have a complete knowledge of the action of the forces which we have studied. But we instinctively extend the lessons which we have gained from partial experience to a region which is inaccessible to us. We are born to act, and action involves faith, trust in the general truthfulness of the system in which we find ourselves.

We are in other words constrained to follow the indications which we notice as to the constitution of self and the world beyond the range of sight, and to interpret them in a larger sense than the facts taken alone warrant.

And so it appears to be also in regard to the different observations which are alleged to shew something of the being of GOD. The arguments from cause and design, from being and conscience, rather point to conclusions than directly establish them. But here again we seem to be made to follow the indications which they give, and to bring from within that which is thus called out. The conclusions are not formally valid, but we do violence to our nature if we do not accept them.

The same constraint attends us in the interpretation of History. If we trace the moral growth of a nation slowly advanced not in accordance with its natural bent, but, as far as we can judge, against it: if a widening lesson of hope, extending beyond its own interests, finds expression in its literature: if the people realise a direct fellowship with GOD and a sense of His holiness found nowhere else: if in the fulness of time One rises from among them, Who, while he satisfies their ideal, gives it a transcending power: if from that time forward the progress of men has been guided by the fuller apprehension which they have gained and embodied in deed of the fulness of that unique Life; knowing what we do of GOD and man, we are constrained to regard the succession of events as the accomplishment of a Divine counsel. Other explanations are possible but this alone is natural. Faith takes the facts and bringing them into a harmonious whole draws out their meaning with the help of larger experience. Exceptional 'signs' find their place in the course of the great drama; prophecies are intelligible in the utterances of men who see the eternal; and the very character of the history forbids us to look for any parallel to the events in which it was consummated.

It may be said, and the assertion is admitted, that this is the judgment of a being who sees but

little of an immeasurable order and may wholly
mistake its import. But it is a final fact of our
nature that we must interpret the phenomena of
human life.

We cannot, from the nature of the case, have
more than indications of the Divine working; and
in this sense Christianity has a world-long confirmation from history. For Christianity, as we have
already noticed, is not an isolated phenomenon. It
has a living relation to all that preceded, and to all
that has followed its announcement. Præ-Christian
history offers us a comprehensive view of the
wants, the capacities, the failures, the aspirations
of men. We find its lessons both in 'the nations'
and in 'the people.' In the history of the nations
we observe the natural unfolding of human powers
in action, in thought, in feeling : in the history of
the People we discern the Divine discipline of a
single race trained to serve and to look for GOD.
In the widest and deepest sense Christianity
crowns the development of the nations and the
education of the People. 'The former,' as it
has been well said, 'prepared mankind for sal-
'vation, and the latter prepared salvation for
'mankind.' We may without exaggeration speak
of the chequered fortunes of men throughout the
ancient world, of their endeavours, their achievements and their defeats, their divinations of their

destiny and their moral overthrows, no less than
of the special preparation of Israel by laws and
psalms and revelations of the growing counsel of
GOD, as one vast prophecy of a salvation to be
wrought upon earth. Step by step the living
sense of a special Covenant with Jehovah, of His
interpositions in their behalf, of His invincible
and perfect righteousness, of His 'conversableness'
with man, defined and strengthened among the
People a conviction of some Divine Coming
among them near at hand, greater and more
glorious than any of old time; and on the other
side the speculations of their doctors on 'the
'Word' and 'the Wisdom' opened the way to
a vision of the self-completeness of GOD, One
but not solitary. Among the Nations the feeling
after truth and beauty and order, in the whole
range of their earthly manifestations, witnessed
to the grandeur, and, it might seem, to the
birthright of man, and dominant tyranny and
corruption and selfishness witnessed to his actual
inability to secure it; and yet among them was
the welcome prepared for one who should be
among them 'a present GOD.'

The Person of Christ standing where He does
in the evolution of human life is in itself the
justification of His claim to be the Saviour of the

world. All that had gone before prepared the way for the apprehension of the Incarnation—of the Birth and Death and Resurrection of the Son of GOD—but there is not the least evidence that any popular expectation tended to create the belief which was fashioned from the facts of the Lord's self-revelation. The earlier experiences of men made the Gospel intelligible but they had no power to produce it. It satisfies and crowns them but it does not grow out of them. Again: the brief records of the Lord's work shew in distinct and harmonious outlines a character which presents the fulness of human powers, powers of action and thought and feeling, of command and sympathy and influence, powers characteristic of man and of woman, shewn naturally with absolute majesty and grace. Whatever had won enduring admiration in earlier times found a place in it. Courage and self-respect, self-devotion and service, were raised to a new elevation and intensity by the habitual sense of Divine fellowship. Tenderness, compassion, meekness, humility were revealed in their true majesty. There is no one who cannot find in it that which interprets and completes and hallows his own personality. The lapse of time takes nothing from its completeness and offers no situation which it is not fitted to meet with calm sufficiency. Peculiarities of time and place and class and work and temperament are lost in that which embraces them all in a universal manhood.

And yet beyond this comprehensive humanity of 'the Son of man' there lies something which is not of man, a conscious sovereignty over men and nature answering to the voice of unfailing knowledge: a vision which sees the truth of things beneath the phenomena of time: a declared separateness from men as well as fellowship with them: an abiding sense of the issues of His mission transcending the highest possible estimate of the achievements of human effort.

The ideal was shewn to the world, and with the ideal power was assured to realise it in many parts and many fashions. For we must remember that the Gospel claims to be 'a power of GOD 'unto salvation' and not simply a declaration of the nature and the will of GOD. The attainment of the ideal has been slow, as we measure time, but endeavour to reach towards it has not been vain. As Præ-Christian history was in its sum a prophecy of the Gospel, so Post-Christian history has been a progressive embodiment of it. As we look back we can see how during eighteen centuries the solid advances of men toward their goal have been due to that which

is of the essence of the Faith: how the failures
of the Faith have been due to the action of forces
which are really foreign to it. We can see also
how the Faith has not only been able to welcome
each fresh access of knowledge which has been
given to man through continuous labour, but
also to grow in meaning and scope under the
ampler light. So it was when the study of the
heavens shewed the relative place of the Earth
in the Solar System, and a truer conception was
gained of our position in space. So it was when
the study of the Earth shewed the relation of
human life to the records of terrestrial changes,
and a truer conception was gained of our position
in time. In each case the new revelation—for
so indeed the Holy Spirit speaks to us—was met
at first with sad fears, and even with wilful
resistance, but now we know how much we have
gained through what seemed to be losses, worthier
views of the immeasurable range of the counsels
of GOD's providence, calmer trust in the inexhaustible patience of GOD's working. And so it may
be even now again. It may be that the study of
human life will teach us to recognise unexpected
connexions and dependences of being, and that in
due time a truer conception of our position in
creation, will enable us to realise a little better
the unity of all things, as a thought, if we

may presume to use the phrase, in the mind of
GOD.

Christianity, in a word, meets and hallows our
broadest views of nature and life. It receives the
testimony of universal history to the adequacy of
its essential teaching to meet the needs of men.
It reaches with unfailing completeness to the
depths of each individual soul. The Person of
Christ includes all that belongs to the perfection
of every man. The Spirit of Christ brings the
power through which each one can reach his true
end. Christianity in a word, to sum up what has
been said already, offers us an ideal and offers us
strength to attain to it.

It is generally agreed that the type of
character presented to us in the Gospels is the
highest which we can fashion. The Person of
the Lord meets us at every point in our strivings,
and discloses something to call out in us loftier
endeavour. In Him we discover in the most
complete harmony all the excellences which are
divided, not unequally, between man and woman.
In Him we can recognise the gift which has
been entrusted to each one of us severally, used
in its true relation to the other endowments of

humanity. He enters into the fulness of life, and makes known the value of each detail of life.

'And what He is for us He is for all men, and 'for all time. There is nothing in the ideal 'which He offers which belongs to any particular 'age, or class, or nation. He stands above all 'and unites all. That which was local or 'transitory in the circumstances under which 'He lived, in the controversies of rival sects, in 'the struggles of patriotism, in the isolation of 'religious pride, leaves no colour in His character. 'All that is abiding, all that is human, is there 'without admixture, in that eternal energy which 'man's heart can recognise in its time of trial.'

This being so 'the Person of the Lord satisfies 'the requirement of growth which belongs to the 'religious nature of man. Our sense of His per- 'fections grows with our own moral advance. We 'see more of His beauty as our power of vision is 'disciplined and purified. The slow unfolding of 'life enables us to discern new meaning in His 'presence. In His humanity is included whatever 'belongs to the consummation of the individual 'and of the race, not only in one stage, but in all 'stages of progress, not only in regard to some 'endowments, but in regard to the whole inherit- 'ance of our nature, enlarged by the most vigorous 'use while the world lasts. We, in our weakness

'and littleness, confine our thoughts from genera-
'tion to generation, now to this fragment of His
'fulness and now to that; but it is, I believe, true
'without exception in every realm of man's activity,
'true in action, true in literature, true in art, that
'the works which receive the most lasting homage
'of the soul are those which are most Christian,
'and that it is in each the Christian element, the
'element which answers to the fact of the Incar-
'nation, to the fellowship of GOD with man as an
'accomplished reality of the present order, which
'attracts and holds our reverence[1].'

But while we instinctively acknowledge the
ideal in Christ as that which interprets perfectly
our own aspirations, for no accumulation of
failures can destroy the sense of our destiny,
we confess, as we look back sadly, that alone, in
ourselves, we have no new resource of strength
for the future, as we have no ability to undo the
past. The loftiest souls apart from Christ recognise that they were made for an end which
'naturally' is unattainable. They do homage
(for example) to a purity which they personally
dishonour. This need brings into prominence
the supreme characteristic of the faith. Christ
meets the acknowledgment of individual help-

[1] *Religious Thought in the West*, pp. 352 f.

lessness with the offer of friendship. He reveals
union with Himself, union with GOD and union
with man in Him, as the spring of power, and the
inspiration of effort. The knowledge which flows
from the vision of the world as He has disclosed
it is not simply for speculation : the glory of the
image of man which He shews is not for contem-
plative admiration. Both are intensely practical.
Both tend directly to kindle and support love in
and through Him ; and love, which is the trans-
figurement of pain, is also strength for action and
motive for action.

In this way believing in Christ—believing in
Christ, and not merely believing Christ—brings
into exercise the deepest human feelings. It has
been excellently laid down by one who was not of
us, that 'the solution of the problem of essence,
'of the questions, Whence ? What ? and Whither ?
'must be in a life and not in a book.' For the
solution which is to sway life must have been
already shewn in its sovereign efficacy. And
more than this, it must have been shewn to have
potentially a universal and not only a singular
application. And this is exactly what the Gospel
brings home to us. He who said, 'I came forth
'from the Father, and am come into the world;
'again I leave the world, and go to the Father,'
illuminated the words by actions which made

known the Divine original and the Divine destiny
of man. The Son of man did not separate Himself from those whom He was not ashamed to
call brethren. He bade, and bids, them find
in His humanity—His 'flesh and blood'—the
support of their own humanity. In His life,
for our sakes, the heavenly interpreted the
earthly. He called out, and He still calls out
in us, as we dwell upon the records of the Gospel,
the response of that which is indeed kindred to
Himself, of that which becomes one with Himself.

The sympathy which is thus awakened by
Christ makes known to the soul its latent
capacities. Again and again our own experience
startles us with unexpected welcomes to the
highest thoughts and claims. Even in ordinary
life contact with nobler natures arouses the
feeling of unused power, and quickens the consciousness of responsibility. And when union
with the Son of man, the Son of GOD, is the
basis of our religion, all these natural influences
produce the highest conceivable effect. We each
draw from fellowship with the perfect life that
which our little life requires for its sustenance
and growth.

I say then without doubt and without reservation that, as far as I can judge, the confirmation

of the Gospel—of the Message of the Incarnate Word—from without and from within is as complete as life can give. Miracles and prophecies considered separately and in detail are not the proper proof of Christianity, but as parts of the whole testimony of experience they have an effective power. Historical testimony originates and commends a religion but it does not establish it. Therefore I say the confirmation of the Gospel is 'as complete as life can give,' for in the end we must make our appeal to life, to life as a whole. We were made for action, made to gain a character, made in the words of the Bible to grow into the likeness of GOD. The final influence of opinions therefore upon the conduct of life may be taken generally as a test of their truth for us. We are so constituted as to recognise the truth which we cannot discover, and life seals the confession of the soul.

It follows therefore, to present our conclusion under another aspect, that the ultimate criterion, the adequate verification, of Revelation to man, in its parts and in its completeness, lies in its proved fitness for furthering, and at last for accomplishing his destiny. That view of the sum of being accessible to our powers which under particular circumstances and at a particular time tends to establish the harmony after which all religion strives, to satisfy man's wants, to carry him nearer to his end, even conformity with GOD, must be accepted as a true interpretation of the Divine will. That view which has this fitness in the highest conceivable degree universally from its very nature: that which is shewn to be most capable of aiding us in our endeavour to attain to the highest ideal of knowledge, feeling, action, under every variety of circumstance, that is, the view which corresponds most completely with our nature and with our circumstances, which interprets our nature and uses our circumstances for the fulfilment of our spiritual destiny, which gives assurance that that which is best in us now is the seed of a corresponding better, must be the absolute interpretation of the Divine will for man. To doubt this is to doubt the existence of GOD and of Truth.

This character belongs perfectly, as we affirm, to the Gospel. If it could be shewn that there is one least Truth in things for which the Gospel finds no place: if it could be shewn that there is one fragment of human experience with which it does not deal: then, with whatever pathetic regret it might be, we should confess that we can conceive something beyond it : that we still *look for another.*

But I can see no such limitation, no such failure in the Gospel itself, whatever limitations and failures there may have been and may be still in man's interpretation of it.

Christ in the fulness of His Person and of His Life is the Gospel. Christ in the fulness of His Person and of His Life is the confirmation of the Gospel from age to age as we look to Him with untiring devotion and seek to see Him more clearly in the light of the fresh knowledge which is given to us.

CAMBRIDGE: PRINTED BY J. AND C. F. CLAY, AT THE UNIVERSITY PRESS.

www.ingramcontent.com/pod-product-compliance
Lightning Source LLC
Chambersburg PA
CBHW031341070726
47496CB00017B/1390